MAN UP!
No Excuses –
Do The Work!

Life Lessons
for
Men Under Construction

By
Demitri C. Kornegay

MAN UP! No Excuses – Do The Work!
by Demitri C. Kornegay
www.demitrikornegay.com

Printed in the United States of America

Library of Congress Catalog Number: 2007930501

ISBN 978-1-60266-611-5

www.xulonpress.com

To Dr. Gomez

I hope you will enjoy this book

Dimitri C. Korn

Sept 8, 2014

Dedication

*T*his book is humbly dedicated with thanks for the sacri-fices, hope for the future, prayers for progress and vigilant, heartfelt, declarations of blessings to-

My Nephews- Clifford Hargett, Jr., George Brian Vaughn, Brandon Hargett, Darryl Lane Kornegay, Jr., Ricky Crawford, Jr. And Sean Hough

My Godsons- Clifton Koonce, Jr., Shawn Fendall, Jr., and Christian Bernard Williams

My Warriors- The Clinton, Md. Boy's Club's 75lbs. Football Team 1999 & Gwynn Park Senior High School's Varsity Football Teams 2000, 2001, 2002, 2003, 2004, 2006 and Maryland's 2005 AAA State Football Champions (We made the playoffs every year because every play somebody did something right!)

My Future Leaders- The Students and Graduates of Men Under Construction

The Sons of Gary Fullerton- Xavier, Jurrell, Jarrett, and Quarnell

The Sons of Eugene Weathers- Jonathan, Jason, and Justin

The Sons of Claude Ferebee- Claude Jr. and Andy

My Father and every man that has been like a Father to me- Elisha L. Kornegay, Elijah Kornegay, James A. Kornegay, Louis V. Kornegay, Alex Preston, Gordon Quarles, Eugene Jackson, Maurice A. Banks, Jr., Samuel P. Taylor, Sr., John Jackson, Sr., Leroy Smith, Sr., and Clifton Hiller, Jr.

My Brothers- Clifford Hargett, Sr., Darryl Kornegay, Sr., Kenneth White, John Jackson, Jr., Maurice Banks III, Rodney Hill, Lance Hatcher, Eric Burnett, Sr., Cliff Koonce, Sr., David Garnett, Sr., Shawn Fendall, Sr., Jason Boyer, Larry Everett, Pierre Ames, James Porter, Russell Holmes, Stewart Alston, Everett Brown, Fred Lexie, Bill Thomas, George Reginald Murphy, Roy Rogers Murphy and Marc Williams.

Capt. Alfred Dooley, Judge Eric Johnson, Ofc. Jeff Kennedy, Ofc. Tom Dolan, Det. Bill Seested, Sgt. J.D. Arnold, Cpl. George Killiany, Capt. George Kassler, Ofc. Jack Kaminsky, Ofc. Charles Carpenter, Det. Victor Kennedy, Ofc. Valentino Jones, Lt. Paul Starks, Garland Branch and Lt. Ezekiel Kornegay.

Reverend Dr. George Roosevelt Yancey, Reverend Dr. David Burhans, Reverend Dr. Eugene Weathers, Reverend Dr. Lloyd T. McGriff

And
Every young man in need of wisdom from his absent Dad,
direction from his missing Mentor, or guidance from his Life
Coach who still wants to read instructions on becoming the
Leader his family, his community and the world needs...

<u>To Whom It May Concern</u>

The first purpose for the letters contained in the book you now hold is to provide, for you the reader, an acknowledgement you were not considered when your missing father disappeared or failed to assume his responsibility. Because of this, an apology is in order. When someone has been wronged, the offense should be acknowledged and pardon should be requested. Please accept, on behalf of responsible fathers everywhere, my humblest regrets the man who was your father will not, or refuses to, see how strong and wonderful you have become and what a marvelous individual you have the power and potential to be. This book will place the young fatherless reader in a more even position with those young men with fathers. Hold your head up. It may not seem like much, but its part of my effort to keep you in the game. Frankly, I feel privileged to be in on the ground floor. You are the next big thing.

Next, in this book you will find, from a Dad, words of encouragement, chastisement, concern, Love, protection, provision, and preparation. This is what fathers do, provide, protect, and prepare. You will read things you should know from a Coach that only wants to see your legitimate success at becoming a man. You are not alone. You are not all by yourself. I'll be your force, that voice that introduces you to the GOD in you and HE will tell you how everything will be alright. Someone does care and this is just one of the ways HE could get to you.

The third purpose, and the hope of this book, is that it will initiate a dialogue between sons whose fathers are with them, stepsons and stepfathers, mentors and their charges. Some day you may be a father and you will need to know these things or, at the very least, point your child in the right direction. Talk it out. My way isn't the only way and the more you know, the more options you will find you have.

The fourth and final reason is a selfish one. My daughter is approaching "courtin'" age and I want her to have a reasonable pool of potential suitors who, armed with intelligence, will be the type of man they would want their daughters to go out with.

Sometimes, it's easy to tell someone else what they should do. Often the answer is no however, when I ask, "Have you ever asked the patient what medicine *they* think they need?" I've been a mentor and coach 20 years and although the subject matter in the chapters you're about to read are the results of questions young men have asked me based on topics they were reluctant to discuss with their parents, I felt there was still room for their voices, not just my advice. With that in mind, I asked, they answered and the results are *"Our Side – Words On the Subjects from the Subjects."*

Read and learn. Read and laugh. Read and live.

Table of Contents

Forward

The blessing of this book, *"Man Up! No Excuses-Do the Work!"* is how it provides a means to empower and equip young boys into the responsibility of young manhood. Uniquely written by one who has labored over 20 years shaping and molding young men makes it a practical guide for self-development. Lack of communication has often served as a barrier in providing healthy dialogue between fathers and sons.

Within these pages we are able to wrestle with the present day challenges facing our young men. Reading these pages will make one more aware of the issues faced by our young men and give suggestions on how to address those issues. Proverbs 27:17 says "Iron sharpeneth iron; so a man sharpeneth the countenance of his friend." When one has completed these pages there will be a greater sense of urgency to address the issues our young men face in today's modem society.

We commend the author for presenting such a needed book in the traumatic times in which we live. This work will serve as a launching pad for future material because it has the pulse of today's society in its grasp.

Dr. Lloyd T. McGriff
Pastor, Galilee Baptist Church
Suitland, Maryland

Introduction

Demitri C. Kornegay, author of <u>Man Up ! No Excuses - Do the Work: Survival Instructions for Men Under Construction,</u> has been able to capture the essence of fatherly advice that all young males need, but, to fatherless sons, it is most essential. Demitri covers everything from the importance of men knowing their history, understanding racism, disappointments, when to fight, dating, spirituality, to death and the pursuit of excellence. This book is packed with passionate advice for young men about the pitfalls inherent in life challenges. It is also filled with the opinions and clear thinking of outstanding leaders like Carter G. Woodson and Dr. Martin Luther King, Jr. This book can truly be a guiding light for all adults who really want to help young men develop positive action plans for the serious journey of life.

The media is full of negative images of men. What are seldom seen are positive examples of young men headed in the right direction. This book provides such insights and with sound goals and purpose.

Demitri asks the right questions and gives the right answers on survival in an unjust world and does so from the perspectives of a concerned father. This book challenges the young reader to understand the impact and the consequences of what he says and how he says it. The author further discusses real friendship versus negative peer-pressure, and how to embrace friendship and control peer pressure.

The writer takes his reader to discussions about the next generation of leaders, while helping him to identify the characteristics of excellent leadership. Demitri completes his personal fatherly journey with insightful discussions about the responsibilities of being a newlywed husband and the importance of fatherhood.

This book is a "must read" for everyone! It is an excellent and insightful guide to understanding, loving and caring for the American male child.

You will appreciate and learn from the very personal experiences of a loving and caring father as he passionately speaks to all the male children in the world.

Cubie A. Bragg, Ph. D., LICW, LPC
Coordinator, Department of Counseling
Bowie State University

The Importance of Knowing Your History

Dear Son,

Everything starts some where so we're starting with History. Everything begins with it. What happened before determines why we are where we are right now. I'll let you in on the first of many secrets. There are reasons for everything. Those reasons may not make sense to us, but something happened, someone reacted to what happened and the results are what some people call history. Always pay close attention to the person that chooses to recite history to you. Is he or she telling you the truth, or are they giving you a version that makes the person doing the talking look good? Does their version of the story encourage sympathy or make you want to assist them in some way? What do they have to gain from telling you?

More about that later. It has been said, you have to know where you've been to know where you're going. If you can take away someone's history, their experiences, you take away what makes them what they are. You disregard what made them unique. Everyone is special and has been put here for a purpose. Some will never discover their purpose and will instead clutter their lives with distractions that keep them from staying on point to accomplish their task. Even in this, there is something to be learned. What, you ask? Those that fail, provide examples of what happens to people that don't complete their assignments. Your assignment is to be successful. We will discuss distractions and their consequences later. Now, we're talking History.

Take away a person's history , what he has been through to get where he is today, and you take away his value, what made him strong or weak, brave or afraid, intelligent or ignorant. We learn from our experiences and the way we choose to address an issue based upon those experiences, makes us who we are. For example, a child that places his hand in a fire and is burned learns what? That's right, not to place his hand into a fire. He will know, from his experiences, fire can produce heat if you get close to it, but it's dangerous to those things that get too close and it destroys whatever attempts to share its space. Fire or intense heat will change whatever comes near it. Learning and wisdom changes the people who get it. People with wisdom learn what is valuable. A man without value can be twisted and talked into doing anything. A man with no values will do anything. Think about it; if you have no value, you are expendable, here to be used by others and there are those people who are constantly on the look out for expendable people; folks they can use, then throw away. We can determine what values you have by knowing what is valuable to you.

Let's look at February. Why? Because in some circles it is referred to as, "Black History Month." While I believe it is a worthy enterprise to set some time aside to focus on the contributions persons of color have made to history, it's also tragic. It started out as a week in the early 1900's by a man named Carter G. Woodson. Mr. Woodson wanted the world in general and the United States in particular to realize African Americans have values and are valuable (A lot of people didn't believe that at the time and that fact made it a whole lot easier to mistreat, beat up, segregate from and lynch folks.) so he developed the idea a week should be set aside to focus on the contributions people of color have made to the world. The intent of "Negro History Week" was to expose the value of the African American to a society that knew little or nothing of their vast contributions. Mr. Woodson's idea blossomed into "Black History Month."

First objection- It's not "Black History," its history, period. Why isn't it taught the same as anything else? How is it your history book can recite so eloquently the adventures of Socrates, Plato, Euripides, and Caesar that occurred thousands of years ago, thousands of miles away, but cannot offer casual mention, at best, about anything that happened just 50 years ago a few miles down Route 95?

We will always find time to study those things that are really important to us. How important is your History to you? Remember, just because it's important to you, does not mean it's going to be important to anyone else. Be prepared for that. On your own, research your History. Find out where the people that look like you came from and what they did when they were forced to address the problems of their day. I'm a firm believer in the more you don't know, the worse off you are. The more you know, the more valuable you become. Look at the problems confronting young men just like you in this country.

Do you want to take a large stride toward straightening them out? Here's how, read. If you can read, there is nothing you can't learn. Learn the truth, then teach it. Teach the truth, the whole truth and nothing but the truth. Parts of it may be ugly, but there will never be anything ugly about learning how a group of people chose to rise above their circumstances and, applying their methods, watching yourself rise also.

What do I mean when I say it may get ugly? Well, watch how ugly some faces may become when I mention Thomas

Jefferson wasn't the only famous white man with black children, all black slaves weren't happy and once upon a time the term "conservative" meant keeping minorities in their place. The confederate flag is a rallying symbol for a group of people who were dedicated to keeping persons that looked like you and I in chains (just imagine how things would be today if those men who originally waved it had gotten their way).

Not too long ago those same folks that waved that flag were convinced they knew how to treat "their nigras" and they didn't need anyone from outside their state meddling in their affairs. They were so convinced, the federal government had to step in and force more than a few Sons and Daughters of the South to be fair or at least tolerate everyone regardless of race. Their feelings were they were within their state and their state had the right to treat it's people in whatever fashion the citizens of that particular state preferred.

As you can see, the good old days weren't all that good, and Crime Analysts are now willing to state if you're black you stand a much better chance of going to jail for doing the same thing a white person will get probation for. I'm saying if a crime is committed, all judges everywhere should heed those four words over the doorway of the Supreme Court. EQUAL JUSTICE UNDER LAW. You know I'm not saying lighten up. You do the crime, you do the time. I'm saying let the hammer of justice fall equally on everybody. The level of justice you receive should not depend upon how much you can afford to spend on an attorney.

When the men that were responsible for the murders of Emmitt Till, Medgar Evers, and countless others were tried in a court of law and walked away after being found not guilty by a jury of their peers, the most "concerned" folk could say was, "It's not a perfect criminal justice system, but it's the best and only one we have." O.J. Simpson puts together an expensive legal defense team and walks and suddenly the entire criminal justice system must be overhauled. It was due an overhaul long before Orenthal James. The words are EQUAL JUSTICE UNDER LAW.

Now, during this particular month, you're going to hear a lot about Rev. Dr. Martin Luther King, Jr. Despite all he had done to help someone else, Martin Luther King Jr. asked that if he were to be remembered at all, that we not remember he had won several Humanitarian Awards up to, and including, the Nobel Prize for Peace. Dr. King said when his name is called he would prefer it not be for his memorable speeches despite the fact his, "I Have A Dream" speech was, arguably, one of the greatest speeches given in the last half of the twentieth century.

Truth be told, the good reverend didn't want to be remembered for his writing, despite the fact his "Letter from a Birmingham jail" is almost required reading in history classes where one wishes to gather the essence of the non-violent civil rights movement.

The fact is, Martin Luther King Jr. said, if you want to remember me for anything, remember that I tried to love somebody. If you must hang a title on me, call me a Drum Major for Peace. Admirable talk from a man that did not live in peaceful times. Admirable deeds from a man whose greatest acts, were in the fact he chose not to respond in the fashion of those persons that disagreed with him.

Admirable foresight on the part of man who himself said, we will either live together like brothers, or perish separately like fools.

Like I said, during "Black History Month," much will be said regarding Dr. King's accomplishments, Dr. King's dream, Dr. King's days, and Dr. King's times. Some may even pose the question, if he were alive today, would he be pleased or displeased with what has become of his Dream? Have we really overcome? And when I say we, I'm not just talking about the

Black folks. What has become of his movement, it's leadership, it's direction, it's focus, his country?

I'll leave those questions to be answered at some other time. For in these precious few moments that the Almighty has seen fit to give me your attention, I'm gonna talk about you.

How do you talk when times aren't peaceful? What actions do you choose when confronted with those that disagree with your carefully thought out, well constructed plans? How will you address the future and, more importantly, what pathways are you opening up and how will you be remembered?

One need only pick up a history book to see what other people, who had considerably less than you or I, chose to do when time, that great recorder of human events, stopped, looked in their direction, picked his pen and pad, and said, "now what will you do?"

Depending upon the obstacle, some reacted violently while others turned tail and ran. Some jumped to the opposition's side, smiling and agreeing with everything their supervisors said, while others just jumped to conclusions. Some went around complaining, while others just went. Everybody did something even if it was nothing at all. Not even realizing that in not choosing, they chose.

When looking back at the 1940's, the 1950's, the 1960's, 1970's, 1980's, and 90's, it's easy for many proud folks to stand up and boast about what they would have done if they had been told to sit in the back of the bus, or enter by the back door, or sit in the balcony, or burn a cross, or sign a petition that would keep a certain family out of the neighborhood or send their children to Christian school because the public school now houses an "undesirable element."

As hard as it may be to believe, as late as 1965, there were people in this country that honestly believed African Americans (called "colored" or "negroes" then) should not have the right to vote for their governing officials. It is with a great deal of sadness I must report to you there are still a great many in the North and South who still harbor those feelings.

Imagine for a moment there was a time when there was no BET (Black Entertainment Television). In fact you could watch television and not see one single black face ever. Schools were segregated, or separated by race, also. Black people went to one school and white people went to another. Somehow, I'm sure it was all quite by accident, the good, new, up to date stuff went to the schools white children went to while the old, outdated items wound up at the schools black children attended.

Poor facilities, poor equipment, outdated books and teachers spending more time keeping the class in order than teaching leads to poor education or no education for students. Poor or no education for the students means they cannot compete with those students who had the better facilities and books with up to date information. This means they will not be eligible for the better jobs because they lack the fundamentals that would allow them to qualify for the better jobs. The better jobs pay more. If you are paid more, you should be able to live better and where you want. (That too, was covered by a system some banks, real estate agents and insurance companies use call "redlining." You see, whenever a black person {who had enough money in the first place to live wherever he wanted to} attempted to borrow money from a bank or get insurance for his car or find a home in a nice neighborhood, the bank would find a reason to say no, the insurance would be too high and the real estate agent would take the black client to an area only black people lived in. A red line would surround black neighborhoods on a map or be drawn through a black person's name and they would not be able to get the same things less qualified white people could. The practice continues although there are laws against it.)

Unfortunately, there are those persons of color who believe if they make more money, they'll automatically be treated fairly. Some even believe the better they entertain, the more fair life becomes. Money becomes the only love. Money is not the root of all evil. The love of money, or greed, is the root of all evil. We'll talk more about money later.

For now, let's deal with you and your place in history.

First question, how do you talk when times aren't peaceful? The Bible says life and death are wrapped up in the words we speak. How many times have you called for the demise of that nincompoop that cut you off on the way to the store? How many words of comfort and well wishes do you extend to those idiots that seem to wait until you're in a hurry to get in front of you so they can show you how slow they can drive? How many cross words have you had with members of your own family simply because they didn't have sense enough to see that you were right and they were terribly wrong? How many times have your children witnessed this? How many times have your children's friends witnessed this? No Children? Okay, how many times has Jesus witnessed this?

A long, long time ago in a galaxy far, far away, I went to an institution of higher education called the University of Richmond. I attended the school on an athletic scholarship. While I was there, there was a football coach named Jim Tait who had a way of addressing people who came to him with gossip. See, whenever someone approached Coach Tait with somebody said something or other about you, him, her, or the light pole, Coach Tait could cut out all that noise with one simple question- What did YOU say?

Such and such is Black and you know how they are. Such and such is Asian and you know how they are. Such and such is Hispanic and you know how they are. Such and such is White and you know how they are.

What did you say? Did you just keep quiet, never realizing that silence is often confused with acceptance, approval or agreement? Did you clear your throat and begin to say something, but then remained silent when you thought about how your response might reflect on your next proficiency evaluation or social standing? Did you shut up and hitch a ride down cop out lane because you figured these folks are ignorant so why even bother to get into an argument with them despite the fact you know different?

What did you say? Better yet, when did you say it?

Did you make a carefully thought out, earnest Christian response to bigotry on the way home where no one could hear it? Did you come home from the party talking about what you should have done and what you should have said? I guess you'll be better prepared next time.

Way back when there were covered wagons and leather football helmets, you know, the 70's? There was a group called Sly and the Family Stone and they had a song called,

"Somebody's Watchin' You." The phrase made a lot of sense. Isn't it funny how things that make a lot of sense force us to use ours? Somebody's Watchin' You. If you believe in an omnipresent, all powerful GOD like I do, Somebody's Watchin' You. Somebody's Always Watchin' You. Picture this, you've lived your life and now it's time to decide whether or not our next contestant, you, get that all expenses paid, first class trip to eternal bliss. Johnny, tell us about our Grand Prize today, won't you?

Heaven! That's right, Heaven! Where everyday is Sunday, your ancestors are waiting to meet you and the sweet potato pies never stop! Heaven! Where Jesus Christ will explain to you all the great things you were in line for if you'd only had a little more faith, and all the questions you've ever had will be answered in the twinkling of an eye.

Somebody's Watchin' you is a statement. The question is, what are they seeing? What are your friends seeing? Why? Because they will be the ones who will remind you, you said weren't going to do that, go back that way, say that, see her, or see him again. What is Jesus seeing? Why? Because chances are when its time to decide whether or not you get into Heaven the last person you want to see is Satan saying, "let's go to the videotape!"

Sooner or later, son, you will have an opportunity just like Reverend King to step up, stand out and speak up though the times, they be a tryin' and when you do, what will the watcher see? What will the listener hear? And what will be the end result of your doing what you did when you did it?

Don't give me that, "I'm too old stuff." The fact that you're still here means GOD has at least a few more things for you to do. Don't tell me you're too young. For the Bible says, "a little child shall lead them." Don't tell me you're too small. For greater is He that is in Me than He that is in the World. Don't tell me you don't have the right connections. For one man or woman with GOD is always in the majority. Sometimes it doesn't have to be more than just a few encouraging words to the right set of ears to set off a chain reaction big enough to change the course of human events.

Second question. What actions do you choose when confronted with those who don't see things as you do? Do you fight? Do you argue? Do you negotiate? Do you surrender? Let me tell you something right now. If you live more than a few days you will find conflict is inevitable but combat is optional. You don't have to fight about everything. Even the Marines have a saying, "Choose the Hill you want to die on."

If you must fight about something, if there must be that thing that will make you raise your voice, grind your teeth and pound your fist on a desk. Let it be something that has to do with respect, dignity and integrity or someone's attempt to deny another of one or all three of those things.

Speak for those who can't. Protect those who can't defend themselves. Educate the illiterate. Practice what you preach, walk the talk, be an example to somebody of what's right with the world. I believe it was Martin King who said, "if you don't stand for something, you'll fall for anything. What do you stand for?

History has shown us the task of changing hearts, minds and habits is rarely accomplished by utilizing the avenues conventional warfare. The face and the fate of this country was changed by the element of surprise. Now a surprise is something that you didn't expect. One can believe or be led to believe that situations are one way, and an event can occur that will reveal to them that things aren't that way at all.

Plantation owners were surprised the slaves didn't want to go on being slaves. Slaves were surprised there were some white folks willing to help them. Educated folks were surprised to find out uneducated folks could learn. Uneducated folks were surprised to find out how much they had been missing. What are you going to be surprised about and how can you surprise somebody?

You know, you'd be surprised at what a whole lot of determined people would do if they're just given half a chance. During my High School commencement exercises, the featured speaker spoke, of course, about how we were young and the sky was the limit. "I Can See Clearly Now," was the Class of '74 theme song and there wasn't anything we couldn't do. The speaker cautioned us not to let anything stand in our way. Not to let anyone who had failed, fill our air with lame excuses that might deter us from our destinies.

To further illustrate his point, he told us of a Kindergarten field trip that was given to some inner-city kids. Now, anytime you hear inner-city or urban, that means Black. This particular group of Kindergartners was going out to the newest airport in the Washington Metropolitan area, Dulles International Airport, and they were all excited seeing the marvelous structure off in the distance grow larger as they approached it. While they were there, now this was some time ago, their guide happened to mention one of the new 747 Jumbo Jets was there and, if they'd like to, they could have a tour of it too.

Well, they toured the plane, seeing all the galleys, spiral staircases, and wide aisles and it just so happened they got an opportunity to tour the cockpit, you know, where the pilots fly the plane from. Watching all the dials, switches, and knobs and figuring everything had to be just right to get something that big off the ground, one little Black child said, "Gee, I wish I was White. Then I could fly this airplane." Another Black child standing beside him, heard him and said, "Hmph, forget that. Just give me half a chance and I'll fly the Hell out of it!"

What will you do with half a chance? I wrote a poem about it. Here it is

> I've seen Trouble roll like thunder....and Pretenders
> hurry from her glance
> While brave souls ventured forward....saying, "Give
> me half a chance"
> Fools rush in and then bow out...as if joining in a
> dance
> But the Conqueror will stand and prove...he just
> needs half a chance
> When all seems lost the Angry blame.....and fill the
> air with rants
> It's then the Wise know all they need....are Faith and
> half a chance
> The Evil lie in wait for Peace....to begin her gentle
> dance
> His partner Harm and good friend, Fear.....consid-
> ering Romance
> Their children Chaos and Despair....began their
> vicious prance
> That's when the Wise, Brave people seized their
> pittance of a chance
> What once was just a whisper...became a mighty
> roar

With constant, unrelenting Faith….Truth evened up
the score

Despair found himself eroding….underneath Hope's
hard glare

And Chaos' parents Harm and Fear…would not
continue there

Then Evil bellowed loudly,…. "I have but one more
trick!"

"Confusion, reign among the throng!" "Let Jealousy
run thick!"

But Evil had not noticed…..that Truth had conquered
Fear

Then Harm and Chaos turned and said, "We're
getting out of here!"

Evil found himself abandoned…as he growled with
his retreat,

"Your Peace is free and clear to reign, but I won't
always know defeat!"

the air had cleared with Evil gone…..another Life
enhanced

All because a few Brave souls said, "Give me half a
chance."

Last question. How will you shape the future and how do
you want to be remembered? I know you have friends that
say things like, "I might not live to see 21 or 18 or even 16
and my response is, "what if you mess up and don't die by
your 21st birthday?" "What if you mess up and live?"

How do you want to be remembered? What do you want
put in the program? What are you going to say when someone
beyond the vale of tears asks, "did you leave that place you
just left a little better than you found it?" Not just for you and
yours, but for folks you didn't know?

That, to me is the true yardstick of greatness. Not how
many touchdowns you ran, or how many baskets you scored,

or even how much money you made. The true measure of greatness lies in the fact, that you were able to put your wants aside, in favor of someone else's needs. True greatness reveals itself when circumstances call a halt to everything and demand you show whether or not you're willing to sacrifice your life and all that you know, to step boldly forward and lay the foundation for those people you will never meet. Greatness says you don't do this because it will make you famous, or rich, or popular, but because it is the morally right thing to do. Greatness does not call for the ability to run fast or jump high, just for the ability to do the right thing, at the right time, at the right place for the right reason and that's something we all will have an opportunity to do.

When you stop to think about it, isn't that why we remember who we remember? Isn't a life lived in that fashion worthy of historical significance? Because of what they did, when it mattered? When does it matter and how? You get to determine that every day you're alive.

Dr. King has had his time and we revere him for his works during that time. These are your times. Will we someday revere you for the work you do now?

If we can, then someday your name will be included when someone speaks of those great someones when he or she says

> Someone sacrificed a lifetime
> Someone died to get you here
> Someone set aside their own dreams
> Someone cast aside their fears
> Someone said for me to tell you
> That you've got a lot to do
> But they also said to tell you
> That GOD will see you through
> Someone said, "Now you're the leader
> And its time to take your place

Listen carefully to the speaker
Here's how you win any race
Call on your faith and intelligence
Embrace the peace knowing GOD brings
But heed the call HE makes to the believer
When HE says, "Arise, its time to do great things!"

Love, Dad

About That Mouth

Dear Son-

What you say and how you say it goes a long way toward what people will think and say about you. For instance, if you think you speak well, go get a newspaper, then tape record your own voice. The playback will allow you to hear how you sound to others and then you can figure out if that is an area that needs improvement. During this little exercise you will also hear how you read. If it's not good, read more and improve it. Everyone that reads well reads well because they practiced. Like that jumpshot, forward pass, or pitch, your reading will only be as good as the work you put behind it. It never fails to amaze me how many different people are impressed when they hear a young man read well.

In quite a few instances, your voice will precede, or go before, you. In other words, folks may hear your voice before they see you. If you speak and read well, more people will look forward to hearing what you have to say. (A brief aside here, always make sure what you're about to say is important enough to be heard. Your grandfather used to tell me, "Never pass up an opportunity to keep your mouth shut." Even Abraham Lincoln said, "It is better to remain silent and be thought of as a fool, than to open your mouth and remove all doubt.")

You know I'm "old school" because "old school" doesn't have old fools. When you get a chance, go to my record collection and get a record out by a group called, "Hall and Oates." The particular song by that group you should be looking for is one called, "Some things Are Better Left Unsaid." Listen to it and then you won't have to play another record by another guy named Tyrone Davis called, "Baby, Can I Change My Mind?" Get the picture?

If you must speak, think first. Down through the ages quite a few people have shown us how misery, destruction, pain, and disappointment ride in behind words that were spoken but not brought out properly. Once the words are out there, they're out there and you can say you want to take them back, but someone somewhere is going to convince themselves what you said is how you really feel.

I've often heard smart people say, "Intelligence is learning from your own experiences, but wisdom is learning from someone else's." History, whether it be world or family, is ripe with disasters that occurred when somebody said something they shouldn't have and the wrong set of ears overheard it. You can apologize until you're blue in the face, but human nature is such that people will remember the one bad thing you said and didn't mean one hundred times and casually forget the hundreds of good things you said that you meant.

As I stated previously, think first before you speak. But you should know there are times when you must speak up and speak out because your silence could cost you. Eventually you will find yourself in a situation where someone will say something, and then wait to see if anyone has anything to say about it. Be very careful here. The speaker may be attempting to "feel" you out or find out what you think. He or she will do this knowing all along that silence, the fact no one says anything, will and is often taken as agreement, acceptance or approval. In other words, if I say this and no one raises a question or disagrees with me, I must be correct and they'll all go along with me on this.

If you disagree with the speaker or have a question to raise about the statement he or she has made, do so in a respectful tone being careful to cite or give an example of how those who oppose his or her position may feel. You are not saying you agree or disagree, you are merely recognizing the fact there are other points of view that may have to be addressed.

Once again, think before you speak. Okay, now here's what you should think about; just before you're about to open your mouth and say something, make sure the words go through three "gates." The first "gate" is, "Are the words true?" There are too many liars in the world and they need you to join the club so they won't feel bad about lying. Speak the truth but don't expect it in return. A seasoned liar is a chameleon (that little lizard whose color changes to match the background he's on so he won't stand out). They say what will serve them, giving no regard to the amount of truth in their statement. Once you tell one lie, a second must be told to cover the first. And so on, and so on.

While we're on the subject here, don't let passion turn you into a liar. Too many people allow "the heat of the moment" to rule their tongues. It's dark in the car, basement, dorm room, or hallway. Strain your ears and somewhere off in the distance you'll hear, "Yes baby, I love you and we'll always be together, just you and me." "Of course I'll respect you." "I've never felt this way before." "You're the one, Boo. You're the one."

A wise man once told me, "Always make your promises in your sober time of day. Never make a promise when your lust is in the way."

Lies told in the dark have a tendency to walk you down in daylight. The last thing you want is to have a reputation as a liar. No one will ever believe what you say because they won't be able to tell when you're speaking the truth. If your reputation must precede you, let it be as a man who speaks the truth.

The second "gate" is, "Are the words kind?" Never underestimate the power of a kind word. You'd be surprised how far a kind word at the right time will go. Just be careful to remember what the motivation is behind those kind words. If they are to compliment a job well done or a nice outfit, period, fine. If they are to uplift spirits by showing the bright side and troubles don't last always, fine. If they are designed to encourage, fine. If those kind words you speak are meant to get you into someone else's underwear, make somebody jealous, or make you look good you're just flirting and a lot of times what you're flirting with, is called disaster.

The third "gate" is, "Are the words necessary?" While some things are better left unsaid, some things need to be said and it's a lot better to receive necessary news from some honest person that cares about you and your progress than to hear it spoken in jest or anger from an opponent. Both instances may reveal facts and facts surrounded by feelings may either cut causing pain, or help start the healing process. It often depends on the deliverer and his intent. Did what you say need to be said?

When you have to open your mouth, use the three gates. It would be nice if your words could get through all three all the time but when they can't, settle for two out of three as long as one of the two is, it's true. If it's true and kind without being necessary check yourself to see if you're flirting. If it's true and necessary without being kind check yourself to make sure you're not being unnecessarily brutal.

Excessive profanity is indicative of a shallow mind that is attempting to impress others, an average mind that has a limited vocabulary, or a sharp mind that is frustrated and has lost control. In any event, we can't have this. Why? Because you never know who is listening to what you're saying when you say it.

Here's an example; you and your friends get on a bus "cussing like sailors" and not giving a **** about that lady at the front of the bus who appears totally disgusted at the loud crude language you and your friends are using. You figure, "what the ****, I'll probably never see that ***** again in life anyway."

The next day the girl of your dreams introduces you to that lady as her mother who had to catch the bus that day because her car had broken down. OR Two days later your mother and the ladies in your building are having the Pastor's wife over for a fellowship and she had to catch the bus because her car had broken down and the Pastor's wife is – OR your boss at your part time job has been so impressed with your potential he wants you to meet his family before he tells you about a scholarship to his college and his wife is- get the picture? All that drama could have been avoided if only you and your friends had watched their mouths.

Just because you use proper English does not mean you're talking like a white person. When someone tries to lay that "you talk like a white man" garbage on you, kindly remind them Malcolm X spoke proper English with proper diction and didn't use profanity and no one ever accused him of talking like a white man. If they persist, just tell them, "You talk like Malcolm Little. I speak like Malcolm X."

Finally, don't say anything you're not ready to back up. In other words, say what you mean and mean what you say. Do what you say you're going to do. That alone will keep you from doing a lot of talking. The Bible says life and death are wrapped up in the words you say. Through Christ, you have the power to speak things into existence. Yet another reason to watch your mouth and think carefully about what comes out of it.

No matter the situation you will find the proper application of the correct words at the correct time without cursing will put an opponent in his place while inspiring admiration for the speaker (you) from the listener (everyone that was nearby that heard you).

Fools speak because they have to say something but wise men speak only when they have something to say.

Love, Dad

Birds of a Feather
(Peer Pressure)

Dear Sons-

Someone once said, "If a man has five good friends in his life, he has led a worthwhile life. I agree, but let's take the matter a step further by examining what type of people those five friends are and what does their reputation say about the man that had them. It is written somewhere that a man is known by the company he keeps. What does your company say about you? You'll come to find, as you get older, this information is very important. Prospective employers, police departments, and government agencies are just a few of the groups that will check not only your background, but depending upon the nature of the job you're applying for, the background of your friends as well. How would it sound to a background investigator if, during the course of his or her checking you out, they were to hear you ran with a bad crowd that no one liked to see coming? This is a major problem. Even in picking your friends, you must examine what your choices say about you. Are you a bad judge of character? Do you and your friends encourage each other to be the best you possibly can, or are you trying to show each other who can be the most anti-social or "act up" the most? Too many times guys do things right now instead of doing the right thing and they never think about how it will effect their future. You're young and you're supposed to have fun, but you should also know that no matter how many mistakes you make, good things are still expected of you. See, I just said it the nice way. To tell it to you the same way it was told to me in a barber shop would be to say, "You're young son. That means we can expect you to do and say stupid things. Just don't abuse the privilege. We're only going to wait but so long for you to wise up."

You've seen sports figures, entertainers, and other people who may consider themselves important because they make a lot of money, roll out with huge groups of hangers-on who don't seem to do anything but hang around the money man or woman. They make up what is known as an entourage. Their job is to tell who ever is bankrolling the good times, they look good, they're real cool, say yes a lot, run errands and answer the phone. Their sole source of popularity and their ability to get girls or guys stems from the fact they're "down" or hang with this month's "Flavor of the Week." They may have started out as "boys" (friends), but now they're working for the bonus baby. The payoff is they get to drive the star's car, live in their house, buy controlled dangerous substances for the group, stand on the stage while he performs, go to awards shows with them or get in the locker rooms and hang out. Carrying your cell phone does not automatically make him your Director of Communications. It starts out as, "I just want to "chill" 'til I get myself together." How cold does it have to get?

Now you, being the star in question, suddenly have a desire to show money and fame have not changed you and you're not too "big time" to still hang with the fellas you grew up with. What you need to understand is, some folks will try to take advantage of your need to show you're still one of the boys. I'm saying you can still be you without allowing yourself to be played like a deck of cards.

While it's fine and okay for them to share in your success, shouldn't they be working to find their own niche or place in this world so they can experience their own? Before you give me that, "Well, my success is his success" crap, remember the words of the Billie Holliday song, "Momma may have and Poppa may have, but GOD bless the child that's got his own."

I know, I've said it myself, "As long as I have, you have." But sooner or later every man has to be able to stand on his own two feet and take care of his own business and family. Being able to depend on each other when times get tight makes us friends. Knowing we can expect each other to do as much as he can on his own before he has to ask for help is what keeps us friends.

You can still be bosom buddies. I'm just saying encourage him to develop his own talents with legitimate value apart from what you do that he can do, and can he find someone willing to pay him for his time and talents. This way he won't get lost in your sauce.

If you're the hanger-on remember just like Mr. Superstar has a life, you have one too. If his gravy train is suddenly derailed why should you both crash? Can you help him through his bad times if your times are just as bad as his? Yes you can as long as you remember and remind him you are both going THROUGH. Don't unpack your bags because you're not staying in Heartbreak Hotel. Tell him he's just a short-term guest at best.

Another part of being a friend is being able to tell a friend when he's about to make a big mistake or fall. It's also about being able to help that friend get back up on his feet after he falls. If we're only friends because I do what you say all the time, I've got news for you, that's not a friendship. That's a dictatorship. Quite often, a lot of friends stop being friends when they start getting on the payroll.

Your friends will make mistakes as you will. One of the reason you're friends should be to help each other straighten themselves out. Sometimes that's hard to do. So many people confuse loyalty with enabling. In other words, if I see you have a problem, and I'm your friend, my job is to help you see it for what it is, deal with it, and then we move on and up together. All too often one friend sees the trouble of another friend and, instead of encouraging that friend to address the problem, they ignore it or smooth over it as if it didn't exist. That's dangerous because in not seeing the problem for what it is and dealing with it, you'll lose that friend and wind up moving on alone. You have to love your friend enough to not just stand by and let him be sorry.

Sometimes, no matter what you do, the friend you love just can't seem to straighten out. After you've done all that you can, you should pray and leave them to GOD. I've found those times when you feel like you're most alone is GOD'S way of saying, "Let's talk." I'm not saying don't be loyal. I'm not saying don't be supportive. I'm saying tell him through your mouth and actions you won't help him kill himself. When you try to save someone from drowning, sometimes they may struggle so hard and panic so much they don't realize you're there to help them and they begin to pull you under with them. If things ever get to that point, push yourself away, tread water, tell them to calm down, do what's right and leave them to GOD. That's right, I'm saying suggest GOD. When he chooses to ask GOD to straighten him out, watch and wait for proof, then welcome him back to common sense land and help him stay straight. The next time he may have to help you. Don't do bad or stupid things just so you can be "one of the boys." Actually, it's been my experience sometimes if you want to start being a man you have to stop being one of the boys. If you're being asked to do something that could wind up hurting someone else just to be a part of the group, is that group really worth being part of? Don't get me wrong, I know everyone wants to belong to something at one time or another and lots of questions about whether or not something is wrong or right come up every now and then. The answer to that is easy. Ask yourself, would I do or say this if someone I respected like Jesus or Mom was standing right beside me. That just made things a whole lot easier, didn't it?

People act like peer pressure is just an adolescent thing. Not true. All of your life, no matter where you go in this society you will be confronted with one or more people who will want you to conform to the actions or wishes of the group. You may even wind up doing so unconsciously (without even realizing it).

Here's an example, look at the now famous "Rodney King" beating tape. So many wonder aloud why one or more of those armed policemen didn't step forward and stop the beating sooner. They say it would have been the right thing to do, so why didn't they step forward and do it? Have you ever gotten on a bus with your friends and they got a little loud? Did you ask them to hold it down out of respect for the other passengers? Have you ever been in a work environment when the boss told a joke and everyone laughed even though it wasn't funny? Have you ever been with a group of people you might have trying to impress and one of them made a less than complimentary statement about a person or group of people who were different from you? What did you do? What did you say?

My point is, all of our lives we will be confronted with some form of peer pressure. From "Give us Barrabas" to "smoking makes you look cool." From you haven't arrived until you live in a certain neighborhood and only wear clothes with a particular design on them, to only allowing yourself to be seen in the company of a certain shade of human beings.

Through it all I'm convinced GOD will always provide us with an ample supply of opportunities to do the "right" thing, while the devil is counting on peer pressure and our need to belong to provide us with enough excuses to do wrong.

Are you willing to stand up for what's right even though it may cost you something, even some friendships and associations? Do you do what you do because it is the right thing to do and not just because you can do it? Do you do the right thing at the right time?

If the answer is yes, then you can handle peer pressure. If the answer is no, then you are going to have work more on becoming your own man and arriving at the proper conclusion of what is right. Remember, politics and popularity are about **who's** right; morality and justice are about **what's** right. When you start to get more caught up in **WHO** did what instead of **WHAT** who did, someone is going to start playing favorites and sooner than later someone that's not a **WHO** is going to do the same thing but they won't get the "special" treatment **WHO** did. That is called unfair.

You are an intelligent young man who, like it or not, is going to be remembered. If you must be remembered, let it be as a man who did the right thing even when no one was looking, and particularly when popularity said do wrong.

Despite our desire to belong, we are all different. Don't be different just to be different. Be different to be better. Like Rodney Dangerfield, you may wind up appealing to everyone that can do you absolutely no good, but I believe GOD will be pleased. I know I will.

Love, Dad

Agendas

Dear Son,

The Random House College dictionary defines an agenda as a list, a plan, outlines, or the like. It would be wrong of me, to watch you grow, widen your circle of associates, increase the distances you travel away from home, and not prepare you for those persons you will meet who have their own agenda, or schedule of events.

Son, if you don't have your own set of plans, rest assured, someone will come along and try to get you to fit into theirs. They may do you a favor, buy you something or provide you with some kind of service and then tell you you don't have to do anything in return. That's crap. If it's not family and sometimes when it is, they'll want something in return and when you start to act like you may refuse, they'll read you the laundry list of all the things they've done for you.

When they do, whoever it is, ask yourself these questions; What do I have to lose from participating in this? What does the planner have to gain? How will this affect *my* future? What can go wrong and who will pay the price if it does? Baltasar Gracian, a 15th century Monk and a very wise man, once wrote that you should never enter into *any* type of agreement with anyone unless they have as much to lose as you do.

Even then, be mindful they hold up their end of the bargain. If allowed, folks will use you for all they can and then throw you away once your usefulness is gone. These words are not meant to provide you with permission to be selfish.

Selfish people are people with small minds and no faith. That is why they hold everything so closely within their grasp and refuse to share. They either don't have or don't believe they have the smarts to get anything else or better and they're way too lazy to get up, go out and work for something new so they guard what little they have, jealously.

Now there are those things you should never share; your toothbrush, your girlfriend, your wife or your underwear. Everything else, with the exception of loved ones and your memories can be replaced. If you look more at what someone does after listening to what they have said, you will begin to gather a very important thing, insight.

Politicians say lots of things, but what do they ever get around to doing? Go to the right church and the people will pray pretty, fill the air with their confessions of faith and then leave the House of the Lord in just enough time to purchase their lottery ticket, buy a fifth of Chivas Regal and bet on their favorite football team.

The real indicator of an individual's true worth and character lies in his deeds. Deeds are the foundation upon which reputations are built. Accomplishments are the mortar of confidence. (Mortar is the bonding agent or cement that holds bricks together.) Once you've done something, and done it well, you establish a belief in your abilities.

There are those that will attempt to enlist your abilities to further their own agenda, often with little or no regard to your plans. Figure out what you want to do and where you want to be, Son. Then figure out what you will have to do to get there and if its worth your soul (here's a hint, its not). Next, visualize what kind of people you will have to deal with to get what you want (here's a hint, all kinds). Lastly, what kind of person will it leave you with when you look into the mirror?

The journey that is life will show you many paths, some worn, some never used. You will encounter many stops, distractions, and diversions. The most important thing to remember here is you choose whether or not to be stopped, distracted or diverted. Everyone does. When you choose or when you choose not to choose, there will be a cost either way. When confronted with a difficult decision, pray on it, put the questions out there and listen for the answer. Although we'll talk more about GOD later, pray on it, then act. Too many pray and that's all. The same Bible that says, "Man ought always to pray," also says, "Faith without works is dead." Develop the faith and then do the work

Every man must establish his own set of personal rules. As a responsible father, I realize I must provide you with a living example of my own to guide you. After reviewing them through the words in this book, you'll decide if they work for you, and add to or take away from them, to develop your own. You decide. Do the research. You choose. You act. That is the only way anything positive will ever be done in your life.

My personal rules are these - Help, with a good heart, not a selfish motive. Always be kinder, more gracious and classier than everyone expects YOU to be. A silent smile confuses evil. No wise man will insult you and no fool can, so do not allow yourself to be tricked into a conflict that is not yours. The best way to avoid a war is to always be prepared for one. Fight only when you must, remembering force is only to be used when the cause is just and the goals are not only clear, but achievable; even then make sure your intelligence is your best weapon and don't hit any innocent bystanders. Have a plan for what happens when you are not there. Always say what you mean and mean what you say so at the end of the day you can look in the mirror and honestly say, "Lord, I did the best I could with what I had and the time you gave me."

When you have done what you can to leave the world a little better than you found it, for people you'll never meet; when you can do a good thing for many and don't have to wait around for their "thank you;" when you can laugh and lose and care and win and stand and fight and kneel to protect and love without pitying and, having done that, still manage not to take yourself too seriously, you will find you know what the beauty of living a full life is.

If you have principles (a set of moral standards you will not compromise or violate) and can adhere or stick to them throughout your journey toward whatever it is that you want, you will be pleased with what you have become no matter where you end up. And if you are pleased with what you have become and what you have accomplished at the end of the journey, then it was a trip worth taking and time, well spent.

Make your own agenda, Son.
Love, Dad

Recognition

Dear Son,

In sports and in life, those people that can, usually award their star pupils, players, or performers with little extras that serve as a way to say, "I appreciate your special talents." Those persons that may not be gifted with special talents but who submit their best efforts consistently should also be recognized. This way, every deserving person receives the proper recognition.

As your father, it is my duty to inform you as you grow older and meet different people from different backgrounds, you will discover that life is not always fair and people with special talents may be rarely rewarded and may not even receive any recognition for their efforts because someone in charge feels the people that are cute, popular, or have connections with people they feel are important, must be rewarded first. Rarer still will be those that receive notice for always doing the best they can do. Once more, because someone else, with their own agenda, will pay more attention to the cute, popular, well connected or the person with the best publicist.

When this occurs, and it will, remember the real power that leads to the confidence you will develop in yourself comes from knowing deep in your heart you have done all and the best you could.

There will be times when you are the best and everyone knows it, but the prize will go to someone who is better politically connected. Remember GOD stands for what's right, politics and people often want WHO'S right. With some people, because you are who you are, that makes you right. This is what is meant when you hear the phrase, "Some people are more equal than others." I'm telling you this now so you'll be prepared when it happens. The true reward in accomplishing a task is the feeling of confidence you gain in yourself. Confidence is nothing more than the assurance you have in yourself or others that, when the time comes, you'll get the job done. If you never receive a single word of appreciation, be thankful GOD gave you the gifts necessary to accomplish the task, put you where you needed to be to see the need and successfully address it, and gave you the wisdom to know HE has blessed you after the job is done.

Look at all you've done and all you can do. The fact is, no matter where you are right now, three years ago if I'd told you then you'd be here right now, you would find it hard to believe. Don't hold the victory party yet, but don't be afraid to congratulate yourself as a work in progress either.

If you haven't realized it yet, time is your most valuable possession. It's the only thing you can't ever really get back once it is gone. Your memory can help you relive the moments, but not those minutes. Whatever you did yesterday was just that, done. This is why I keep saying we must make the most of every second, every word, every job, every play, every relationship.

If you knew this week you would never see a loved one again after today, how would you act? I get the feeling you would make sure the last thing they heard you say was, "I love you." Now I've got to throw a chill into you. How do you know you haven't seen that loved one for the last time? The truth is you don't.

That having been said, why not give Mom and the women in your life flowers, just because? I can tell you now, they'll appreciate them more because it wasn't a special occasion. I am by no means an authority on women (truth be told, most men that think they are, aren't) but I do know this; a woman likes to know you think about her, even when she's not around. Now don't stalk her or call her every five minutes, but a card or a flower from you on an ordinary day of the week will make you a Hero. It also shows you're wise enough to recognize everyday GOD lets you have them in your life is special to you. That will make you special to them.

I hate to say it but it's just that simple. This is how you make your life special and it is the people that make life special that are remembered and recognized. It's time for you to shine, and in doing so, confirm what you may have suspected but I've always known, **YOU ARE NOT A MISTAKE. GOD WANTED YOU HERE AND HE HAS SOMETHING GREAT FOR YOU TO DO.**

HE gave me the honor of being the one to tell you. A lot of us wanted to, but HE blessed me. So it's my job to tell you now that no matter what it is, study it, practice it, rehearse it. When it's showtime, it's SHOWTIME! The fact you've made mistakes just makes your comeback all the more spectacular. You can do this. Make the change for the better and watch how many others that you didn't think were watching you, follow your lead.

Do everything from now on as if you were going to sign your name to it because that's your designer label. It's a "You" original. Your work will be remembered for its quality.

A long, long, time ago in a galaxy far, far, away, when I was in college I was amazed at the number of people who were so upset they no longer "ruled." Here were kids who were used to being the smartest in their school, or the cutest in their school, or the most athletic in their school having a mental meltdown because they weren't the cutest, smartest, or strongest anymore. This is what happens when you are the best where you are. When you are the best where you are, it's time to move to the next level. Some people you meet will stay where it's safe and never venture outside of what they know. They'll talk loud and walk tough, but they're afraid. That is why they stay so close to home.

Big sturdy ships that are safely docked at their piers are indeed, safe. But that is not what they or you were meant to do, stay safely at the dock. There is an ocean of life out there complete with storms, smooth seas, sharks, mermaids, and treasures and while you can get there from here you can't get them from here. You have to be willing to go get them. If you don't, you'll spend your life talking about what you should have done.

You've got to go to the level where everybody that used to be the most this and the best that is starting out new all over again just like you. Things they used to just naturally "get" they now have to work for. There was this one girl, Debra, who was so upset the guys weren't kissing her feet at college the way they used to at her high school where she had been "Homecoming Queen," "Most Talented, " yadda, yadda, yadda. Well, one day a friend broke it all down for her when he told her, "You may have been the Homecoming Queen back home, but now you're at a school with a lot of girls who were Homecoming Queen. In other words, the level of competition has moved up and you're not the center of attention anymore. Recognize, adjust, adapt and overcome or go home and have a good cry. Either way, deal with it."

You've often heard me say college provides us with the opportunity to see what we're made of. You'll go to bed when you want, get up when you want, eat when you want, wear what you want, study when you want. You'll also compete with people from across the world and this is when putting your best effort into everything you do will count the most. That is why I suggest you start getting used to doing it now.

When you have done your best and the prize appears to have gone to someone else, honestly review your performance and pinpoint where you made your mistake. That learning experience will prove to be invaluable. If you made no mistakes at all and it was just a "beauty contest" (a competition they say is based on talent but the winner already knew they had it because of their connections) celebrate your efforts, thank the folks for the opportunity to show what you could do (remember, this is our chance to show class) and move on to bigger and better challenges. One day they'll come begging and you may not have time for them.

You have and will face the pressures of high expectations and going where no members of our family have gone before. There is also the Grandfather you never met that had the desire to better his family's circumstances. He put that desire in me and now I'm putting it in you because he told me everything I'm telling you.

We have family members that have abilities and talents, but are still wrestling with themselves over when to step up and apply themselves. Some are afraid and can't handle the slightest rejection. That is why they keep their talents in small familiar places where only a few can keep telling them how good they are. They'd rather receive nothing but constant praise in a corner than take the chance on growing and expanding to unbelievable heights with constructive criticism. Some tried and initially failed. Burned once or even twice, they've shut down and now they hold the world responsible for their troubles. When you take responsibility for your life, you take control of it. Complacency is a comforting drug. It makes you lazy and says, "let's settle." You're not here to settle, you're here to succeed.

Some people may witness what you are being recognized for and become angry because they feel whatever it is you're getting should have been given to them. This is called jealousy. What is for him will be his when and if he works hard enough for it. Jealousy is nothing more than selfish anger over wanting what somebody else has because you haven't taken the time to appreciate what you've got.

What is for you will be yours in time. The story is told of a young man that spent every waking moment waiting for Christmas to come because then he knew he would get presents from his friends. He spent so much time waiting for that one day, he never went outside to enjoy the Spring's fresh grass or honeysuckle flowers. He spent so much time daydreaming about Christmas he ignored Summer's warm evenings and Fall's golden afternoons. He spent so much time thinking about what he would get for Christmas he not only forgot his own birthday, he forgot the birthdays of the people who were supposed to give him his presents and he forgot to call just to say hello. When Christmas came, he didn't get anything because he never left the house and everyone thought he had moved. He only realized when it was too late all the other things he could have been doing until the day he looked forward to got there. What's coming will get here. Focus on improving what you can while you're waiting for its arrival. Moral of the story – Don't be impatient, be efficient with your time.

Someday you will relay this information to your son. I Love You and we will talk again.
Love, Dad

Racists

Dear Son,

The time comes when every responsible father in America must sit down and talk to his children about the issue of race and racism in this country. Like most interpersonal issues, its better to talk about it calmly with foresight than to wait until the issue is thrust upon you and catches you unaware. Most of the time the subject is treated like an illegitimate child no one addresses it until they absolutely have to and then the subject is dealt with either too long or not long enough and that depends upon who brought the subject up in the first place.

The United States is a nation of immigrants. The people who were here first, were the Native Americans. The reason they are called Indians is because the people that traveled to this country from Europe were searching for a faster route to India where luxurious silks and spices were. While the argument still goes on about who got to what we know as the Caribbean first, whoever got there called the inhabitants West Indians and the title continues to this day. The name was also applied to the Native Americans in the continental United States.

What does this mean? Often during the course of a heated exchange concerning race, someone is usually told to go back where they came from. If everyone went back to where they came from, the Native Americans would be the only ones here.

Many of the people that came to this country came voluntarily and were seeking a better way of life. Many African Americans however, were kidnapped from the continent of Africa and then sold to people who would ship them to the United States where they were supposed to live out their lives as slaves. Attempts to enslave the Native Americans failed because they were familiar with the areas they worked in and could run away. Imagine being taken so far away from home you couldn't walk back and wouldn't know which direction to start walking in if you could. All you know is you must now work in a strange land with strange food and you must learn a new language because no one knows yours. You're also given a new name because your name is too difficult to pronounce. You're treated like the livestock you used to own. You could be sold to someone as near as next door or as far as a five day walk and you had no say in the matter. Your family could be split up and sent in different directions. You had no rights. You could be whipped, have body parts chopped off or killed if you attempted to run away. Such was the life of the slave in early America.

There are those people that would suggest slavery was not all that harsh and some slave owners were good kind-hearted people, but I've yet to hear of any those folks volunteering to take the slaves' place.

Not all African Americans in this country were slaves, but the majority were slaves. These were humans being treated like animals. Slowly, over the course of time, things changed. People in this country began to understand others that did not look like them were just as human as they were. That went for Jews, Irish, Asians, Latinos, Italians, and Caucasians too.

Laws had to be written and rewritten to ensure everyone, regardless of how they looked, was treated fairly.

I'm sure you've heard it said somewhere by now life isn't fair and as soon as you figure that out, it starts becoming more fair. You should also realize by now all you have to do is breathe, and somebody is not going to like you for whatever reason. You haven't done anything to anyone, but someone said something, about somebody who looks like you, and quite often, for people who are too lazy to think, that's enough. There are Black people that have been told all their lives by people they trust, "if you want to get half as far as the White man, you're going to have to work twice as hard." There are White people that have been told all their lives by people they trust, "Black people are lazy, slow-witted, and want something for nothing." Every group seems to have a "you know how they are" about everyone else.

Listen carefully, everyone is an individual and should only be held accountable for what they say or do, not for what someone who looks like them did twenty years or twenty minutes ago.

I can remember being 15 and traveling with my friends to stores, sporting events, parties, or just plain walking down the street and suddenly, it appeared as though people were afraid of me. Now remember, I was big for my age, but their fear didn't make sense to me. I never harmed anyone and that has never been my intent. But all I had to do was walk into a room, step on an elevator, or walk across a street, and women started clutching their purses, people started locking their car doors and police officers started giving me nasty looks.

Needless to say, at first I was confused, then angry they would think I was a thief or a thug. I know you have friends who have tried to glamorize "thugdom," but let's get real, who do you know, other than other thugs, that wants thugs in their house? Everyone knows one, and everyone thinks they know what a thug will and won't do. Some of your friends say they are thugs because only thugs showed them Love. Please. Were they showing Love or cultivating an opportunity to get you for a favor later? Use your head, son. A thug is a murdering thief who'll use any excuse to commit any abuse. It's always somebody else's fault. Some would even have you believe they get all the women just because the women like "bad boys." Bull. Just remember this, women always consider it their own personal privilege to change their minds. And they'll change "bad boys" like they change nail polish. No matter how good she looks, you don't need that type of woman or the drama she brings with her. Plus, "bad boys" grow up to be "sad men" if they grow up at all, but we'll talk more about that, later.

As I said, the thought that people who didn't even know me, would lump me in with a criminal crowd made me angry and hurt my feelings. It then dawned on me how I would never be my own man nor could I ever control my own life if I allowed someone else's perceptions or beliefs about me to control my emotions. Strangers don't make me anything. Mad, sad, or happy. You make you. Get it? Good. Now you say it. They don't know you. To control the situation you, must first learn to control yourself.

Just like they didn't know Martin King, Benjamin Mays, Elijah McCoy, Medgar Evers, or Malcolm Little, they don't know you. Those guys were all your age once, and they had to go through crap that was much worse than anything you or I will encounter and if they triumphed, so can you. Imagine having to walk in the back door or sit in the balcony because some folks felt you weren't good enough to be in their presence. Add to that when they did need a seat, YOUR seat became their seat because neither you or your comfort were considered worth valuing. That's why I give you and your boys the blues about riding in the back of the bus or sitting in the back of the class.

There was a time when people that looked like us had to sit in the back if they were going to sit anywhere at all. That kind of treatment was so rampant, we got to the point we just started automatically going to the back of things. That's a dangerous place to become familiar with. You start getting used to that position, and if you have any pride at all, you try to make what was down, up. Good becomes badd, stupid becomes great, mad becomes a lot, and hope becomes dope. Prison attire becomes either an aspiration or a fashion statement. You and your friends are better than that. Once you figure it out, it will start to radiate from your insides out. Then others will get the idea you're about something because you'll speak and dress and carry yourselves that way.

Understand this son, hatred of Black people does not always have to come from the White man. Some groups have watched others hate them so long, they've taken up hating themselves. Don't look so surprised. The story is told about two lines of people buying ice in Harlem on a hot day. A Black man was selling ice and a White man was selling ice. The White man's line was longer. When someone asked why, he was told because the White man's ice was colder.

How do you progress when you look at people who look like you and think failure, bad, poor or sorry? Why did you have to wait so long for your cheeseburger at the fast food place in one neighborhood while at the same franchise in another neighborhood the food was delivered fast, hot and with a smile?

I tell you why. Because life is about expectations and acceptance. It's what you expect and what you will accept. If you expect to be treated like a man, but will accept being treated like a dog, put on a flea collar because a dog is what you'll be. If you expect to be dealt with fairly, but will accept anything someone tosses you, get prepared for a life of leftovers.

If you expect to expect something, without properly preparing for it, you have no choice but to accept what you get. I'll explain. You want the best? You must be the best. How do you become the best? I'm glad you asked. Think, study, prepare for your opponent's response, and envision your success. You want top shelf treatment, you've got to give top shelf performance. Work hard. Work harder. I believe it was Vince Lombardi who said, "The harder you work, the harder it is to surrender."

Stupid ideas about you being inferior because you are whatever you are, are the result of some people surrendering to ignorance. Accepting that you are inferior for whatever reason, be it a mental beat down or physical brutality on the part of a policeman who believes everyone that looks like us is a thief, is surrender. You are not here to surrender. You are here to succeed. Don't ever apologize for being a Black man. Where we come from being a Black man means knowing the many contributions people that look like us have made to civilization despite burnt crosses, poll taxes, and trees that bore strange fruit. Don't you dare apologize for being a Black man. For us, being Black men has meant proving we were better than our circumstances. It means knowing hate is a fool' s toy and a weak mind's excuse. If they are afraid of you, of us, they must learn to get over it. We only strike fear in the hearts of those who would do wrong.

Sooner or later you will witness what is commonly referred to as "white privilege." You will notice certain people getting instant service with a smile while you get slighted with a scowl. Give the person the benefit of the doubt. Perhaps their feet hurt or their underwear is way too tight. Be patient but don't be a punk. A closed mouth smile bewilders aggression. If you're angry, don't show it by raising your voice or becoming disorderly. Ask to speak to a manager, get names and inform the responding party their employee's conduct is unacceptable and you would like to know what they intend to do about it.

When you're standing in line to pay for clothing, you can't afford to mentally "fade out." Observe how the person in front of you in line is being treated. If they paid with a credit card, did they have to produce identification? If not, neither should you unless your name is not on the card. If a security guard demands to see what is in your bag, make sure you have witnesses, then demand to see the manager. Get names. If the bank won't cash your check and you have an account there, see the manager. Some people have to be forced to respect you. Don't let their being disrespectful cause you to become disruptive. They will use your losing control as an excuse to arrest you. How many times must I tell you, he who loses control, loses.

In our present times, we must be mindful there are people who don't mind being racists, they just don't want to be called racists. This being the case, I would be wrong if I didn't properly prepare you for them. We'll discuss police encounters at another time. We're talking about retail establishments now. Salesclerks can't talk down to you if your vocabulary far exceeds theirs. If someone persists in attempting to belittle you, remember you don't have to spend your money in this place. When you pay them, you are keeping them and their rude behavior in business.

Be proud of yourself and don't forget you represent strength, wit, foresight, and perseverance. I was once told to "scare people to death with my intelligence." You will enable yourself to lead your family to the next series of successes if you do the same.

Love Dad

Intuition

Dear Son,

Let's discuss briefly the power of intuition. As you may already know, the Baptists call it the, "Spirit of Discernment." Others call it their Guardian Angel, while the rest just say, "something told me not to go over there," or "something told me to leave that woman alone."

It is that warning signal that tells you to look up so you can see what you should duck; that thought that makes you wait an extra three seconds at the traffic light as it turns green when a truck runs the red light. Intuition is the voice that tells you it is time to leave the party while everything is calm and then you hear there was a shooting right after you left.

It allows you to gauge, measure or sense the feeling of anxiety in a room or tell when someone has a hidden agenda. It's the feeling you get when you get the feeling you're being watched. Insight is all these things. How is it developed? Good question. For some, it is a gift that comes naturally. For others, an acquired talent that improves through the years. The first step is to observe life around you and really see what it is showing you. For every action there is a reaction. Figuring out reactions is one thing, trying to figure out why the action took place in the first place is another indeed.

Just as jumping jacks or squat thrusts are exercise for the body, prayer and meditation are calisthenics for the soul. You must discipline yourself to focus on what you know to be good, honest, and true and then figure out where you are. Put yourself in a quiet place, listen to the silence and see what it tells you. What stays in your head and why?

Prayer consists of five things; Praise, Thanksgiving, Intercession. Asking, and Forgiveness. In praise, we give honor to the Creator not only for all that has been done in ours, and other's, behalf, but for who HE is. We should always be thankful for what works because we can use it to address the things that don't. Remember WHO to be thankful to because it's bigger than you or I. Intercession is merely going to someone on behalf of someone else. In other words, you are putting in a good word for someone you care about, to someone who can help them. Lining up your actions and thoughts with the will of the Creator entitles you to ask for whatever you want. Just remember you'll receive it in HIS time, not yours. Even when we are trying to do our best, we sometimes offend. In seeking forgiveness for our actions, known and unknown we recognize our own imperfections and the need to hold ourselves in check. It's hard to think you're all that when you realize you have to be forgiven because you weren't all that.

To meditate, you need only to pause mentally, be so still you can almost feel the breeze caused by the movement of the Earth, and focus on something as simple as the waves coming into the beach over and over under the light of a full moon. You must discipline yourself to seize the moments but if you do both, pray and meditate, you will find your intuition is sharpened. Exercise your mind by working out simple addition problems in your head. Start with things like 2+2=4, then 4+4=8, 8+8=16, and so on and so on. Move to subtraction, rounding off numbers and reading to improve your vocabulary. Witness the change in the seasons and their effect on those around you. Think about others and what makes them happy. Now, ask yourself where you want to be 10 years from now and what are you doing right now to put yourself there? If 10 years seems too far off, think about 5 years, and 3 years, and next year.

Once again, all these things are geared toward helping you to exercise your mind. True power is the ability to envision something in your mind and make it someone else's reality. You must be careful with this. Envisioning evil or conspiring to do wrong against others to satisfy your own selfish motives will eventually bring you pain or shame, or worse, pain and shame to those whose opinion you hold dear. Use your head. Think, where will my actions lead and decide if it's worth the price.

No matter where you go or what you do, there will always be an opportunity to do the right thing. Listen to the voice that tells you what it is and then take advantage of that opportunity without taking yourself too seriously.

Instinct, insight, intuition, the spirit of discernment, Guardian Angels and extra sensory perception all seem to have the same thing in common. (1) They're there to help you and (2) they can't unless you decide to listen. The choice is yours as are the rewards or consequences you will have to face as a result of your choice.

What do you want, son? And what do you think those who are around you want from you? With prayer and meditation, time and insight always reveals these things.

Love,
Your Father

Disappointment

Dear Son

Y ou are destined to experience those times in your life when things won't go the way you wanted them to. It can be anything from an athletic contest to a love affair; from a big test in school, to a promotion at work. Life brings tests, trials and, triumphs and the result of these, depending upon your outlook, can leave you with your feelings hurt because the outcome was not the one you had hoped or planned for. This is known as disappointment.

There are many different ways we may choose to address disappointment. Some choose anger. Anger is a dangerous dance partner that will encourage you to lash out at anyone in the vicinity up to and including those folks that didn't have anything to do with your current situation. Anger will poke and prod you to work yourself into a frenzy until you fallout exhausted, with shame and depression your only remaining companions. You're ashamed of what you said and did, and you're depressed you chose to handle the situation in that fashion.

Some choose depression. Depression is a dark map designed to take you to places and things you really don't need to be and see. Think about it. It's like the domino effect. The moment you choose to invite depression on the scene, it says let's go find some way to get over me.

There's legal liquor, illegal drugs, physical exertion, and violence. It's been suggested the older you are when you choose to be depressed from your disappointment, the more people you hurt. Here's an example. You're disappointed and then you choose to be depressed. Your depression says, "let's go get drunk and forget our troubles." You do this, and after hurting the feelings of the few that really care about you, you get behind the wheel of a car and ruin the lives of strangers.

You didn't mean to bring harm to anyone other than yourself, as it was after all, your pity party, but now you've brought misery to people you don't even know. Of course you wish it had never happened and you should have thought more clearly. Jail cells are full of people who wished they had thought more clearly.

The young are not exempt. How many times has someone that cared about a child had their feelings hurt by a decision their young one made when they were depressed? Here's an example. A child wants attention and he or she doesn't get it. They are disappointed. They choose to be depressed. Depression suggests a number of attention-getting methods from swearing to vandalism and other antisocial acts. Be they young or old, they are choosing to hurt others because they have been hurt.

How then, are we to address this guide named depression? The same way we address anything life ushers to us, with our brains. By correctly using our thought processors we come to realize disappointment is a part of life, but depression is a choice.

It's a fight, but you simply must choose not to be depressed. Depression far too often attempts to convince us to list all the wrongs done to us, both real and imagined. I would strongly recommend we make a mental note of any perceived harms done to us, file them away to be examined at another time, and immediately start counting our blessings.

Like oil and water, depression and blessing counting don't get along. Depression can't take you down a dark road if you're counting that blessing that says, "but I can see the light." Depression can't call anger to help make you lash out at others when you're counting the blessing of a sound mind that realizes it's not their fault, they're just doing their job, or it wasn't my turn. Depression says get mad. Blessing counting says get smart. Depression says, "let's go get stoned." Blessing counting says, "let's go get straight."

By counting our blessings, and you do have some blessings (most of which we all take for granted until they are temporarily lost), and then earnestly evaluating why we didn't receive the desired outcome, we can determine what needs to be fixed, adjusted, or discarded, do it, and move on.

You are going to be disappointed. Why? Because everything won't always go your way. You may choose not to be depressed by realizing life is a constant state of being. Who and what do you choose to be? Make the choice. Do the research. Confirm that choice by making an informed decision, then prepare for the role you have chosen.

As long as you're learning something, it's not a wasted experience. Remember, lack of preparation is preparation for failure. As I've told you many times before, it is all about choices. You can, when you get knocked down, choose to roll back and forth in the dirt of despair and whine to yourself and anyone that will listen; or you can pick yourself up, dust yourself off, figure out where you made your mistakes, and attack the problem again.

Be motivated, not mad. Be inspired, not inhibited. This way, you'll wind up successful and not sorry.

Love, Dad

When You Should Fight

Dear Son –

There will always be those people that will disagree with you about something. In fact it is written somewhere that conflict is inevitable, but combat is optional. You will be called upon to decide which is which. Here are some things that will help you figure it out.

You are my Son and I love you. Wars and battles have been fought over oceans of time so that people could be moved from place to place and things have been arranged just so by our Creator to make sure you would get here now. You are not a mistake. There is a reason for your being here and you should know I believe it is not to die over something as trivial as a stepped on foot, a stolen parking space, an unsafe lane change, or a mean glance. Enough have died from this foolishness. As you venture further from home you will receive the opportunity to meet people who have not lived as you have lived or shared the same experiences you have. The boys that did not receive enough attention at home now do things that will scream for attention in public. Some will intentionally do wrong because, as the song says, "Seems Like I Gotta Do Wrong For Someone to Notice Me." They believe this, so they seek attention by gaining some sort of reputation. You've heard all the speeches about low self-esteem you need to hear. If my own self confidence is faulty, I'll pick own you, chump you, or make you feel bad so I can feel good about me. Never attempt to elevate yourself at the cost of someone else's self-respect. It will only focus a brighter light on your shortcomings. You must instead learn to work to better yourself. Be it mentally, there are plenty of books to be read. Physically, your body as it is, is a gift from the Creator; what you do with it is your gift back to HIM. Spiritually, you must establish your own personal relationship with GOD. Study to improve and show yourself approved.

Once again, I apologize for not being there physically, but this is HIS way of making sure I could still speak to you. What exactly am I saying? Sun Tzu, an Asian General who lived over 1500 years ago said, "The best way to avoid a war is to always be prepared for one." Do as I instruct and you will be prepared.

You have heard me say on more than a few occasions, the more you know, the more valuable you become. With the expanded knowledge you gain from reading and learning, you will find your horizons also expanding. The circles you will find yourself traveling in, because of your increased knowledge, will direct you further away from the paths of self destructive fools who are too afraid to die alone. These are the people who feel they must fight about everything.

When confronted with an opponent, they will look at you but you must look *in* them. Quickly size up his or her abilities (what are their strengths) and, review the terrain (where do they want you to fight them). Obviously, if they are confronting you they must have done some planning before hand. This must be where your preparation takes over. That is why your grandfather always told me to know where the working exits are in any room you enter.

Fighting, Force, is only to be used as a last resort and almost never should it be the first consideration when you are faced with opposition. Even the military, professional fighters, know no force should ever be used unless it is over-whelming and has clear, definite goals. If you must fight, ensure every possible advantage is yours. Do not allow your anger or pride to goad you into a confrontation. Anger is a dangerously deli-cious dance partner that is very jealous. She commands all your attention and will keep you from talking to your good friends whose names are GOODWILL, UNDERSTANDING and PATIENCE. She will dance with you until you fall exhausted. She will then leave you with her friends, SHAME, REMORSE, and sometimes, TOTAL LOSS.

Pride is Anger's associate that whispers things in your ear like, "that fool must not know who you are. She can't do that to you. You don't need to know this stuff. You already know that. Can't nobody tell you nothing. If I was you, I'd set these people straight." Then Pride brings Anger over. We've already discussed what happens then.

Mario Puzo in his book, "The Godfather," wrote about the type of people who rush about begging to be killed. You must learn to recognize these people so that you can side-step them thus allowing them to keep their appointment with destiny. They are the ones who listen to Pride when he tells them they can do whatever they want whenever they want to whomever they want. Upon meeting them, smile partially (show no teeth), nod, and step aside. If he asks you if you think something is funny, tell him, "only that GOD continues to love us both despite our faults."

There will be those that will spit in your direction with their eyes. Upon meeting them, smile, say, "God Bless You," and move on. Always use your peripheral vision. They may have conspirators. Surprise the surpriser and you'll retain the upper hand.

It is a well-known fact the average person only uses 10% of his or her brain. It is said geniuses use 12%. This means 88% of our gray matter is just sitting there waiting for something to do. Use it by playing the "what if" game. As in what if such and such does this or such and such does that. Using the other 88%, formulate a solution to the problem that does the least amount of harm to the greatest number of persons. This is avoiding war. This is always being prepared. Through carelessness or lack of preparation, anything can be taken.

Never go looking for a fight. If there must be that thing you must fight about or for, let it be life and the dignity, integrity and respect therein. Don't allow anyone or thing to take yours or anyone else's.

Just as there are different ways to laugh, dance, or smile, there are different ways to fight. If you feel you have been wronged by a business, there are proper steps to take to file a complaint. Acting out only gets you arrested for Disorderly Conduct and Disturbing the Peace. Get names. If the offending party won't supply them, do the research and write a letter that contains, places, dates, times and descriptions. This is called documentation. In your letter to the boss of the boss of the offending party, don't forget to include the manner in which you reasonably want the issue resolved. When confronted by an opponent, if you can leave the confrontation without having exhausted all of your resources and in doing so, can maintain and renew what had been depleted or used up, you have won the battle. You must be careful to make sure your victory is not a Pyrrhic one. Of course I'll explain. Pyrrhus (pronounced PIE-russ) was a Grecian king that lived in ancient times. His armies defeated the mighty Roman legions on land and at sea but in doing so, he lost everything. That is why when you win something and the cost is too great, it is called a "Pyrrhic Victory." In all conflicts, weigh the cost. Is victory worth this?

Speaking of this, when quarreling with a loved one, stay on point and only debate the issue at hand. Nothing is ever accomplished by saying things that are meant to hurt feelings. Words that cause pain are hard to take back and are remembered long after the argument is done. Are the words true? Are the words kind? Were the words necessary? This is where wisdom comes in.

I have just shown you how to become and remain a winner when confronted with an opponent. History is always written by the winners and what isn't written down, will be forgotten. You have history to make. I am proud of you. Go and make me prouder.

Love, Dad

The "N'" Word

Dear Son –

Many times I have been asked and told, "what's your problem with the word, "nigger?" "It's just a word. You trying to act all sophisticated and high and mighty. Sure, people that don't look like us use it and we get mad, but when "we" use it, we just acknowledging our folks. Don't be so serious. Stop trippin'". Some folks even attempt to take the shame off by spelling it "niggah."

My response is, picture this- a white man sees a black man, turns to his son and says, "that's a nigger." The same man then turns to his daughter and says, "that's a nigger."

The black man, upon hearing the white man explain to his children what people who look like him are to be called, has a choice. If he remembers the adage, "I am not what you call me, I am what I respond to," and chooses not to answer when addressed in such fashion, he retains control of his own destiny. How? Because he is determining how he will be addressed.

If, however, he looks at himself and allows someone else to determine who and what he is, and says, "well, I guess I am a nigger." "My friend over there who's black, well, he's a nigger too. My daughter and her playmates are niggers.

My teachers, my preachers, my doctors, my plumbers, my friends, my niggers. "

Now you tell me, who's fooling whom? I don't care how hip you try to sound or how "down" you think you are, that word was initially used to separate and degrade a people and attempts by the historically ignorant to transform a slur that meant inferior into a term of endearment depending upon who uses it, insults our seniors and evokes feelings of embarrassment for the speaker from the listener who knows better. And it doesn't matter how you spell it.

I challenge the reader to name one other ethnic group that openly in mixed company, and on recordings that go on sale to anyone, uses an ethnic slur as a term of endearment.

I further challenge the reader to seriously examine the history of this country, the way that this country has treated people of color, and the struggles for dignity and respect those same people of color have had to fight for, in order not to be referred to as a nigger.

Doubtless, you will encounter those who will suggest, well that was in the past and we're living in the now. To them I say and say loudly, it is no wonder no one respects you and you don't respect yourself. Only a people that know its full history will prosper. Those that don't will drift through the seas of time floating like so much waste in a toilet. Some say when you know better you should do better. Well, isn't it time to know?

When do we learn African Americans will never be accepted or respected as equals with anyone foreign or domestic until 1) we don't care what you think of us because we care what we think of us and 2) we form our own independent economic power base that forces the consumer and those that wish to be elected to come to the table to deal with us on a consistent basis (don't tell me *we* can't, look at the Asians, the Italians, the Jews).

It is only then that the vicious term that has been applied to people who look like the little girls that were bombed in churches in the name of white power, marchers that were fire-hosed and chewed by dogs in the name of "state's rights," young women who couldn't walk down a country road for fear they'd be raped by a group of white boys in a pickup truck in the name of fun, and young men who couldn't walk down that same road for fear that same group in that same pickup might decide they need to become part of the tree that bears strange fruit in the name of God and country, will be tossed onto the scrapheap of disgrace only to be used by those willing to incur the wrath of a decent and upright society.

Only your God or your parents can name you. Accepting the word "nigger" then attempting to remove its sting by claiming there is a different meaning when the individual using it is an African American is the same as a Slave being told by a Master not to go off the block. So you climbed over the fence and out of the yard, but you dared not cross the street. You took the word and changed it. Why aren't you intelligently independent (read bold or brave) enough not to take or accept the word, period? What are you afraid of?

Finally, when the subject arises I politely tell everyone I come into contact with I regard use of the word "nigger" by whites an insult, and the use of the word by blacks a notification of that speaker's surrender to mediocrity, inferiority, and hopefully, less than popular opinion.

I know the struggles of my parents, their parents, and their parents before them and for me or someone that looks like me to use or apply the use of that term would be an unconditional surrender to those who hold the belief people that look like us are lazy, stupid, have no worth and only eat watermelons and chit'lins, no matter the color of the speaking offender. I won't do that and neither should you.

Love, Dad

MONEY

Dear Son,

Despite what folks will tell you, money is not the root of all evil. Like many other things, that saying has been rearranged either on purpose or quite by mistake and like everything, to determine which is which, it all depends upon who the speaker is at the time. First Timothy, chapter 6, verse 10, in the New Testament of a book we know as the Bible tells us it is actually greed, or the love of money that is the root of all kinds of evil.

You will meet and/or see people who will do anything for it, believing cash will get them respect, power, love and happiness. The thing you must remember here is money is like a car, a vehicle. Money will give you access to many things and places. Although it can take you there, there is no guarantee you will be happy when you arrive.

The Devil makes it easy to confuse monetary wealth with respect. Turn on your favorite video program and you'll see young men just like you with gold in their mouths, on their wrists, and around their necks, riding around in expensive cars and flashing cash in front of nearly nude women. If you could hear what the young men were saying, you might be led to believe they feel they can do anything at anytime to anyone solely because they've "got it goin' on."

What have they got "goin' on," really? They allow someone else to decide for them what is valuable, and then without bothering to do the proper research fly half cocked into a "I gots to go for mine" mentality. If you can rhyme over a drumbeat, you can be a rapper. If you can carry a tune in a suitcase you can be a singer. If you can shoot a basketball or run a football or hit a baseball, you too can be a role model. Not.

The facts are, all the aforementioned parties are nothing more than entertainers who entertain well enough to generate interest from a bored public that is anxious to be the first to know about the next big thing. The only reason people that would otherwise have nothing to do with them are willing to become their best friend for life is because that same public might be willing to pay money to hear or see them.

Remarkably, some folks with close to no talent at all become stars, while those with the real gifts are known to but a few. If the latter receives any attention at all, they are usually the overnight sensation that has been waiting in the wings for twenty years. But they find they have learned a great deal more than instant notoriety could ever teach them. They are the ones who learn their faith, persistence, and determination are what got them through. They are the ones who know they can deal with anything that comes their way because their trust was in the Right One. They are the ones who "wouldn't take nothing for their journey" because their "journey" gave them the one thing instant success cannot, experience.

The first group has the right backing or publicity and provides proof talent is no longer a requirement or prerequisite, for superstardom. Surrounded by an entourage or posse that swears undying loyalty as long as the cash holds out, they go to what they're told is the best this or the best that. As your grandmother would say, "they get new." Suddenly, what was good enough, isn't anymore and everyone that comes close, must be impressed.

Manners are for the moneyless and they can do anything they want because they're rich and their lawyers can work it out. Interested observers such as you or I may watch and wonder why those "one hit, one game, one success wonders" don't make this "once in a lifetime opportunity," a lifelong dream? Why not? Because someone once said money only magnifies what you always were. Why don't the nouveau riche, or new money, learn some class befitting their new prosperity? Aristotle Onassis, one of the richest men that ever lived said, "Money cannot buy class, but it can purchase tolerance for its absence." The simple fact of the matter is, people tolerate classless rich people because they hope they'll throw some of that money their way. (For examples, see athletes, movie stars, and/or recording artists in night clubs, restaurants, or airports.) Bear in mind, this is not an indictment against all athletes, movie stars, and/or recording artists, just those that don't know how to act.

How should you act? It's simple really, just treat people like you would want to be treated just a little nicer, always remember where you come from, and do what you say you're going to do. Never forget that you are only responsible for how you treat people, not for how they treat you. Keep the right amount of distance between yourself and a fool.

Money can buy you a house, but it cannot buy you a home. Money can purchase someone's company for the evening or even a weekend, but it can't purchase love. It can buy you a piece, but it can't buy you peace. Money can buy you attention and acclaim, but it can't buy you respect or dignity. Incidentally, the fact some folks will do anything for money has cost them their respect and dignity. They quote Malcolm X out of context and say things like, "by any means necessary," or " the ends justify the means," or " I gotta survive." Those who base their income upon the misery of others often find themselves the victims of their own dismay. They will soon be hunted and fall prey to twice the pain they gave out.

Ignorance is no excuse. Jails are full of people who say they just didn't know. But jails are also full of people who laugh at the "suckers" who "play it straight." This is nothing new. You have a choice. You can be legitimate and relaxed or you can hustle and keep looking over your shoulder. This is nothing new. Aesop wrote 600 years before Christ, "Better bread and water in comfort, than cakes and ale in fear."

When your ship finally does come in, remember it was Les Brown that said, "If you make enough money, someone will find something cute on you." Case in point, we've both seen some women swoon over guys who, based on their looks alone, if they were pumping gas or delivering mail instead of singing or acting, they wouldn't get the time of day. Because they do what they do, and make the money they make, they are supposedly worthy of our unerring adulation. Be careful of the "new" friends you make and the price tag that comes along with their presence. Remember the words of Barry White: "I spend money. Money doesn't spend me."

A man pays his own way and the way of those persons he is responsible for. He provides food, comfort, clothing, and an atmosphere in which learning can exist for those who must depend on him. He provides the example of how one should conduct himself under pressure or during times of plenty, and his vision for the future includes preparing loved ones for a life without him.

Realize the more you know, the more valuable you become. In other words, be willing to learn how to do something so that people that can, will pay for your time to do it. Gather the necessary experience and learn to do more, so that you place yourself in a position to be paid more. When you start out, be willing to exchange low wages for great experience. You may know you are worthy of higher salaries but until you prove it, you're just whining.

Once you have proved it, if your supervisor is worth anything at all, he or she will ensure your pay reflects your value and your potential. If they don't, don't complain. Continue to gather in as much knowledge and experience as possible, then search elsewhere for businesses that will better appreciate your time and efforts. No one should know you're leaving until you have to give your two weeks notice. Take no parting shots and burn no bridges because you may find yourself coming that way again. Remember, always a class act!

Set up a budget for yourself that establishes a long-term savings account (for retirement/emergency funds), a petty cash fund (for movies, etc.), and weekly living expenses (groceries, gas for car, etc.), in addition to paying your rent/mortgage and utilities (electricity, gas, water).

First, take one tenth of whatever it is you get or earn, be it your time or money and give or devote it to the Church of your choice. You know I believe GOD has given us gifts and giving the tenth or "tithing" is our way of exhibiting we recognize where our blessings come from. When you tithe, you're helping the Church continue GOD'S work.

When you purchase your home, that's right, when. You should know your credit rating (that's the reputation you will have established for paying your bills) had better be great because it's a fact there are those lenders that look for excuses not to lend money to prospective home buyers that happen to be from a certain ethnic group. Sure there are laws and every so often some housing group will conduct undercover tests to tell us what we already know, but you should know your job is to make sure you have all your ducks in a row. Make them run out of excuses for not loaning you the money.

When you're old enough, you can do what you want but I only use the few credit cards I have for emergencies. When you get yours, use them sparingly and then pay them off as soon as possible. Always pay considerably more than the minimum fee and don't miss payments. This is how you establish good credit.

Remember whatever car you purchase will require preventive maintenance (oil change, tune ups, tires, antifreeze, brakes, etc.). While we're on the subject of cars, read carefully the financial agreement and the percentage of interest you will purchase your car for. Depending upon how much you'll actually drive, it might be better to lease the car.

Interest is merely the amount or percentage you pay for using someone else's money or what someone pays you for using yours. You pay when you have a credit card. The amount you have to pay can be as much as 25% of whatever it is you buy. Here's an example, if you buy a pair of shoes for $100 with a credit card at 25% interest, you pay whoever issued you the card $125. If there is a monthly fee, you pay more. You're paying for the convenience of using that credit card.

You get paid when you have a Certificate of Deposit (CD) or a Money Market Fund. In either case, you are paid a percentage of whatever amount you have in that particular account. Obviously, the higher the amount, the higher the interest you'll be paid. Check with the bank you're doing business with because they always have a minimum amount you have to deposit for at least a certain amount of time and there will be a substantial penalty (fine) for early withdrawal (if you take your money early).

It has been said, when you are poor or just getting by, you work for your money. When you are rich, your money works for you. That is the basis for stocks, bonds, money market funds, etc. You invest in a business and if it does well, you share in the profits by being paid what is known as dividends.

Don't forget taxes, federal, state and local, and whatever other contributions (social security, health insurance, life insurance, dental, vision, and prescriptions, etc.) are taken out of your paycheck. What they say they'll pay you is called the gross. What you get after all the above is taken out is called the net. Some of it you get to choose if its taken out and some of it, you don't.

Now imagine you're your mother, it's Christmas time, and you and your brothers and sisters want a Play Station apiece, complete with the most expensive games, a pair of Nikes, a pair of Timberlands, a leather jacket, and a Tommy Hilfiger shirt. All this in addition to paying the regular monthly bills. If you're mature enough, you understand the pressure your mother is under. If you're just a child, all you know is what you want. Where's Dad? See the importance of taking care of those people you are responsible for?

Congratulations! It's up to you to go and find out more about the financial world, where you come down in it, and what you want out of it. It is, after all, your money. If you make enough, you can hire someone to handle your money for you. Allow me to warn you about that by saying this, there are those persons out there who are honest when it comes to handling other people's money and there are those who are not so honest. One group obviously has no idea how hard you worked to get what they're about to take or give away and the other can only work as hard as they can with what you give them. Either way, they both come with a fee. My advice to you is free because I'm your Dad and this is my job

I Love You.
Dad

Dating!
(For readers age 16 or older.)

Dear Son,

One of these days, you'll tire of hanging out with the fellas or going out alone and decide its time to go out on a date. How do we do this? Well, a date can be a group, two couples, or just you two.

In order for this to occur and since you want her to go out with you, it falls upon you to do the asking. Now asking for a date has been done in many ways but the most successful way that has yielded the best results is verbally (speaking out of your mouth). You could write a note but imagine your embarrassment if she just doesn't say no, but Xeroxes copies of your heartfelt request she spend an evening with you. (It has been done.)

While we're on the subject of embarrassment, let's review some of the times it would not be a good idea to ask for a date. Never ask a woman who is with someone at the time. Chances are, that guy she's with is not her brother or even her cousin. If you ask her in front of her girlfriend or girlfriends, once again embarrassment capability is high.

I have found it's best to ask your intended guest for the evening to step to the side and out of listening range for prying ears and then, after having practiced what you're going to say, make the inquiry. There are those legendary individuals who can fire away and every word will sound like music to the ears of the lady they're asking but, if you're like me, play it safe and work things out ahead of time. It'll keep you from making a fool of yourself. (Incidentally, women don't like fools unless they're going to use them for finances or transportation. Hence the name, fool.) Don't try to be too cute. Don't try to be too slick. Don't try to be too cool.

It's okay to be nervous. In some circles, you can win quality points for working it into the conversation during the asking. Such as, "Look, I'm fairly nervous about this entire exchange (dazzle her with your vocabulary but don't bore her with an English lecture), but I'm willing to set my anxiety aside for the opportunity to spend an evening with you." If she's interested, she may ask, "where?" My advice is to be prepared with a number of places you think you'd both like to go to. This may call for some research. What kind of movies do you like? How do you like to spend your spare time? Have you ever done this or that? Make it nice, conversational. Don't make it seem like you're taking her downtown for a few routine questions at Headquarters.

If she says yes, don't do the Florida Seminole wardance, or loudly pronounce yourself "Pimp of the Year." Merely smile, make the final arrangements such as where to, when, etc. A very important note here, if your boys, friends, crew, or partners are nearby after you've set the date, do not walk back over to them grabbing your crouch or any other such nonsense or you will have blown the deal. Most self-respecting females won't like their reputations being made sport of by you or your friends.

Sidebar here. If the impossible occurs and she says no, smile, say, "Some other time, perhaps," and excuse yourself.

Don't call her names or talk about her shoe size. What I'm trying to say is, when my friends and I were dating we had a rule we always adhered to. The rule, "Always a class act." She dresses like Lil' Kim and talks like "2 Live Crew?" Be a class act. She drinks like Dean Martin and dances like a Great Dane in heat? Be a class act!

Question. Are you the kind of guy you'd want your daughter to go out with? If not, why not? Work on that because you're going out with somebody's daughter. The truth of the matter is when you go out on a date you don't know what to expect, but you should always know what things you hold yourself responsible for. You are responsible for the safety of your date. You open doors for your date. You talk to her in an effort to discover what her interests are. Make her feel she is the most vibrant interesting creature in the world this evening. You do not stare at the Honey with the 38 double DDs who has just announced this is your lucky night if you can lose the ball and chain. You are a gentleman, such a classy one that when she remembers the date she had with you, she'll remember you were the one date she had that knew how to treat a lady (even if she didn't act like one). Make yourself a tough act to follow without going broke or proposing.

Wash up, smell clean and dress stylishly. Don't be a slave to fads and, unless the intent is to surprise, let her know what your plans are for the evening or afternoon. If you're going dancing, when you dance fast, don't dance wild. You may hit or kick somebody. When you dance slow, be careful where you place your hands and try not to get too excited. If you brought her, pay attention to her. Make her glad she's there with you. She's your guest for the evening and even if she doesn't know how to act, remind her as quietly and as courteously as you can where she's wrong. If she goes postal, suggest this may not have been the best time for you to entertain this evening and perhaps you should take her home.

Do what you say you're going to do. This means if you tell her you're going to call her, in the name of Alexander Graham Bell, tell her when and then do it. Whole talk shows, women's magazines and "Waiting to Exhale parties" are centered around why didn't he call when he told me he would. In other words, always give your date the utmost respect. She may have the rep of Rebecca of Sunnybrooke Farm but when you get her alone she may turn into Vanessa Del Rio. For your own safety and hers, no sex until you've both had checkups and even then, abstain for as long as you can. It's too dangerous these days and besides that, there's still the chance you may wind up becoming a father way before you're ready.

Clarence Carter sang, "Take Time to Know Her, It's Not an Overnight Thing." Truer words were never spoken. Some women will throw themselves at you when its late at night and the music's right. After you finish ego tripping and before you do something rash or end up with one, ask yourself if its just your day or if its just you, today? Remember, this is somebody's daughter here. Things can get hot and that's when you have to think with the head between your shoulders.

Never force anything. You don't force yourself on anyone. No means no. Period. If, upon your arrival to her residence you find she 1) is not there or 2) has decided not to go and hasn't got a reason, you my brother, have just joined the ranks of the stood up. Be calm, it happens to the best of us. The Spinners sang a song about, *"spent all that day, fixin' up to go somewhere. Thought I was late, and I found she wasn't there. I guess I'll find, love, peace of mind, some other time, but I still have today-"* When this occurs don't mope down the street with your hands in your pockets kicking cans, go out and do whatever it was you were going to do just without her. I went to my Junior Prom all by myself and had the time of my life. I fast danced with the ladies whose dates were too busy trying to look cool to dance and had charming conversation with those unescorted young ladies until they announced they wanted to slow dance.

Dating should be fun, not an ordeal. There are those things called "Blind Dates." Somebody somewhere feels you and some woman with severe emotional trauma would make a perfect match. I'm not saying don't go, but be afraid. Be very afraid. Odds are you'll meet a positively delightful young lady who is a joy to be with, or a church going dominatrix who's still angry the fiancé she met when they were pen pals in jail ran off with her mother. (If she looks familiar to you its because they all were on "Jerry Springer" last week.) If she's a drama queen who loves to make a scene, don't buy into it. Let her make her scenes all by herself. You are a good man and she will miss *you* when the evening is over. While you're enduring, remember the "class act" rule.

Date people you like and that like you. Don't brag about your dates or try to impress your friends with descriptions of torrid evenings of passion. Try to avoid the "Sammy Sausagehead" role. This is the guy who wines and dines Miss-Got-the-Body only to find out she's somebody else's "Booty Call" as soon as he drops her off at home. For further information, go back to the description of fool.

Take it upon yourself to enjoy your "free agency" as long as possible. If it's a game, let all the participants know you're just playing. That way the truth can't be thrown up in your face. What I'm saying is, be honest with all parties concerned. After all is said and done, when you're ready to get serious with one, *you* won't feel like you've missed anything and, when choosing "*the* one," you'll make an informed decision.

Love, Dad.

Love, Heartbreak, and Marriage

Dear Son,

Let's talk about love. What is it? That's fairly hard to say. To me, love is more of a verb than a subject. In other words, it's easier to say what it does than what it is, so bear with me. A wise man once said, love can make fools or geniuses of us all. Love makes life harder or easier depending upon the situation. For a more accurate description of what love does, try the New Testament book of First Corinthians, Chapter 13 in the Bible. Some versions will call it charity, but its love.

Some call it being "sprung," having your nose wide open, or being "whipped." Whatever you and your boys choose to call it, the first steps are those warm feelings you get all over when you think about her. It's the smile that comes over your face at the mention of her name and the excitement you feel just walking beside her. It's the little twinge of doubt you quickly put away when you think to yourself she could do a whole lot better than settle for me.

Yep, that's how it starts. Friends may not be able to see what she sees in you or what you see in her, but then, its not really their business now is it? Some women can walk into your life and before you know it, you're grinning like a Cheshire cat every time she comes around and you're showing off for her. Like I said, your partner may not feel the vibes you do, but remember, what's treasure to one man may be trite to another.

Now, you appreciate the woman's existence and you want to spend more time with her. Take your time with her. If she's interested she'll let you know. If she's not, she'll let you know that, too. Don't let it get to the point she has to put out a full page ad either way. You know a guy who met this fine honey at a gym way back when he was single. He moved smooth and all the vibes were right. They arranged a date to go out of town to a Virginia State University Homecoming, you know, to get to know each other. Something came up and he had to get in touch with her to tell her he would be an hour or so late. So he called and called to make sure he didn't blow their first date together. It turns out she felt he called too much, and broke the date.

Now you know that guy is me and I'm just trying to keep you from experiencing the same devastation. I'm not saying don't call if there's a change in plans, just don't call every hour on the half hour.

Take your time. She's not going anywhere. If she does, maybe you're lucky. A relationship is like a car accident, the slower you go, the less damage you do. Strong things that last over the course of time are those things that are built on firm foundations and that takes time, partner. One of your Uncle's favorite sayings with regard to women is, "Start out like you can hold out." In other words, the same thing it took to get the woman, will be the same thing it takes to keep her. Why? I'm glad you asked, because that is what she will come to expect. That is the foundation YOU laid when YOU started this thing. Your only option is to make it better. Let things get worse and you'll find yourself being excused and replaced.

Sometimes, no matter what you do or how hard you try she won't dig you. There you were imagining life with her in a big house with beautiful kids and a dog and things just didn't work out. It won't seem like it at the time, but life goes on. Birds will continue to fly and chickens will continue to fry. Take one night, put all the sad songs you can think of on your stereo, cry your little eyes out and then, with the breaking of dawn, move on. Even the Bible says weeping may endure for a night, but joy cometh in the morning.

Believe me, everything will be alright in the morning. Maybe not tomorrow morning, but sooner or later one morning is going to come and everything will be alright. If she didn't want you, it's her loss. Don't go on a shooting rampage. Move on and let her see what she did herself out of. Frank Sinatra once said, "The best revenge is rampant success."

Just because you're alone does not mean you have to be lonely. I know it will seem like everybody has somebody but you and the radio is playing nothing but love songs, the television is showing nothing but happy couples and all the world has "a special someone" but you. Don King once said, "I didn't serve time, I made time serve me." Take this time that you find yourself by yourself and work on becoming a better you. Surely there is something new, like a foreign language, you could learn. Volunteer your time to some worthwhile event. Remember, there will always be someone somewhere that may need your skills and abilities. Visit a Veteran's Hospital or tutor someone. You're not running for Sainthood or public office, you're doing your part to make the world you live in, better. In doing this, you will find the more you focus on assisting others, the less you'll fixate on your own ailments.

When you're with the one who appreciates your company and time, get to know her in all seasons. Not just winter, summer, spring, or fall, but *her* winters, *her* summers, *her* springs, and *her* falls. Does she do self-destructive things when she is happy or sad? What does she do when she's bored or confused? When she's angry does she try to make everyone else angry too? Can you trust her? Can she trust you? Time answers all these questions, Bucko. Ignore the answers because they aren't what you want to hear and you will pay and pay dearly. Then, if and when you do finally escape, you'll find yourself asking yourself the same two questions everyone who has ever been in a bad relationship asks themselves when they're out and looking back, "What in the world was I thinking and why did I stay so long?" Some people make good friends but not good spouses. In other words, some friends we make we shouldn't marry but make sure you marry your friend.

Realize that you both were raised in different households therefore, holidays, family gatherings, and family relationships have the potential to mean different things to you both. For instance, your family may not like to get together during the holidays for whatever reason (they may have never gotten together), where her family can't seem to wait for some occasion so everyone can see each other. She'll go and if she gives a you know what about you, she'll want you to come along too. If you don't go, you'll find yourself not wanting her to go either. This is a prescription for disaster. Work on it and work it out. That means talk. If you bite your tongue thinking things will change after while, you're going to wind up pouting around with your bottom lip poked out.

If you love her, I mean really love her, you'll want to see her happy all the time. Fact of the matter is, you'll want to be that thing that makes her happiest. You'll live for her most full-throated, heartiest laugh. When you love someone son, what's important to them is important to you because they're important to you. You'll have to love her enough to want her to be the best she could ever be even if that means she'll be leaving you behind. You see, love is about sacrifice. Love says I don't eat until you dine. Love says I don't sleep until you rest. Love says I'll tell you about Heaven, while I walk with you through Hell. Love says you and yours becomes mine and ours and of all the things you have to wonder about in this world, you know that GOD put me in your life so we could show others how HE meant love to turn out. Love makes us vulnerable, but because we're in love we're willing to take that risk they can hurt or make fools of us.

If I can't have you, nobody can is a child crying over a possession. We're talking honest to goodness grown up love now, son. When you do decide to love decide to love with class. If you don't have any, go get some. Then if she wants to leave, let her go. You're not her father. When it comes to adults, you can't make anybody do anything they don't want to do and resorting to physical force is a sign of a frustrated weak mind that can't logically reason the problem out. It's only a waste of time if you learned nothing from the experience. If she doesn't want this, no matter how well you had it all worked out, it wasn't for you. There is someone better and the sooner you let this one go, the faster you'll get to the right one.

Be that thought that causes a warm rush, an easy hidden smile, and a soft, almost inaudible sigh instead of a smirk, rolled eyes and an expression that says I'm glad that fool is gone. What I'm saying is, be a good memory, not a hard time. That's loving with class son.

Now, let's talk responsibility. You've been committed, that's right committed, to this woman for at least two years now and you can honestly see yourself with her and her alone from now on because every other woman that might wander into your path will be a distant third, at best, behind her because she takes first AND second place. Tyra Banks, Carmen Electra, Eva Longaria, Gabrielle Union, Esther the Video Vixen, Pam Grier, Halle Berry, Vanessa Williams, Nia Long, Marissa Sorvino, Beyonce, Asia Carera, Jenifer Lopez, Janet Jackson, Rosie Perez, Cory Everson, the Tennyson Twins and Lucy Liu are all dismissed.

Now its time to ask yourself some rough questions. If she gets sick, really sick will you take care of her? I mean emptying bedpans, wiping sweat from her brow, reading to her, feeding her, washing her, caring for her? When she cries, does it tear your heart apart? Will you protect her? If you have a ten, is eight of it hers?

Don't bring outsiders into this. Don't have a "standby" on the side. I know you've been around your uncles and cousins with all their loud talk for the crowd about how it's a poor rat that only has one hole. I suppose that would apply if one considered oneself a rat but that is not what you are here to be. Can you do that? Not be a rat? Can she trust you? Can she depend on you?

All aforementioned answers must be yes before proceeding to the next level. Research. Ask her how she feels about children and how they should be raised. Ask her how long she plans to work. Imagine her with twenty more pounds. For that matter, imagine yourself. Can you deal with this? Can she? Who will do what in the house and how do we plan on keeping the house clean? Assume nothing, ask everything before you get caught up. We've already discussed the importance of fatherhood so remember, your children will base their conduct on what they see you do with their mama. If you're never there, that teaches too.

Next, go to her father with a plan. Here's where I am now and here's where I see us in twenty, fifteen, ten, five years. Why? Because no man is going to invest his love and time into being a father to his daughter only to give his blessing to some starry eyed fool who'll whisk her off to a sorry existence with no plan, money, or job. In other words, my son, be prepared or at least have the potential to give her a better life than she would have had at her daddy's house.

After that man to man talk and presumably with his blessing, go to her with ring in hand and a request for her future. Don't get so caught up in the hype you forget you're there to get married, not be the social event of the season.

If you're the head of the house, she's the heart and the children are the hub. Listen to the woman, know your principles of leadership, and lead by example. You may not be the preacher of a church but you are the Priest of your home. This means the spiritual health of YOUR family is YOUR job. We have seen too many families where Mom will take the lead but its Dad's' responsibility.

She will be the heart of the home. This means nothing will seem right if she's not happy. She'll bring the warmth, comfort, and sensitivity if you bring the love, concern, and attention. You give her a house, she'll make it a home. You give her food, she'll make it a meal. Bring her your heart, she'll give you her world. She must feel protected and provided for. Even if she can fend for herself, she wants to know you'll put yourself out there for her. Do this and you'll never be sorry.

When they come, all events that occur in the house should center themselves around the sound mental, moral, educational, and physical health of the children. You and the wife are your children's examples of how to act. Do your best to raise them right so when you're gone, they can legitimately take care of themselves. Their room should be the one with the most sunlight because they are the brightest part of your future. That's why children are the hub of the home.

Your lifestyle should reflect the faith you have in your family's future. In other words, every action you take should be executed with the welfare of the family *you* created in mind. Don't drink, smoke or waste away your paycheck when you know you have children to send to college. Your vacations should be excursions where the children can learn by expanding their horizons.

This is what you're saying when you say you are in love and want to get married. You're ready to be responsible. You're ready to be held accountable. You've got to be ready to work, pray, protect, provide, prepare, love, console, advise, teach, earn, direct, discipline, and plan. You will make mistakes. When you do, admit them, seek pardon from the appropriate parties and move YOUR people forward.

Love, Dad

The Importance of Fatherhood

Dear Son,

You have reached that point in your life where you now have the ability to create life .Note I said you have the ability. Possessing this particular ability is like possessing a gun, just because you have it, doesn't mean you should use it, for if you choose to use it carelessly or carefully, disaster could still be the end result. More on that later.

You now have a deeper voice, hair on your privates and wild thoughts that have the potential to betray you. Although the thoughts are normal (most of them, anyway) you, like every other young man before you, must learn to control your response to these thoughts. Like everything else in life, it doesn't matter who or what is encouraging you to take action, what matters is your reaction.

As you look around you, there are many people and things urging you to lose yourself in "the moment." That is not a wise thing to do. Moments, much like the actions we take within them, are things we can't take back. Like time, once it's gone, it's gone. In order to successfully navigate through these minefields we call adolescence, manhood, and life, we must pick our moments carefully and with foresight.

Foresight is merely the ability to look ahead and plan for the pitfalls, obstacles, curves and detours that may lie ahead. The better prepared you are for them, the better off you'll be. Lack of preparation is preparation for failure. Now I realize you can't possibly foresee everything that will come your way, but quite a few of the things you will encounter will never change. There will always be someone who, for whatever reason, has decided they do not like you. Everything you will want in life will come with some sort of cost attached. (Frederick Douglass said over 100 years ago. "Although we may not get everything that we pay for, we will surely have to pay for every thing that we get.") Hearts will be broken, dreams will be shattered, underdogs will win, chickens will continue to fry and birds will continue to fly. Someone will see in you things you don't see in yourself, while others will underestimate you on sight. Like I said before, what matters is your reaction to all this. While we all go through pretty much the same thing, what makes us unique is the fact we go through these things at different times. Everyone I know has found themselves better off when they have fully thought through what the impact would be on their lives were they to take what they thought they wanted when it was presented to them.

Phrases such as, "Oh, what the hell," or "I'm SO weak," or "I just don't know what got into me," "we just got carried away," or "just this once," are usually the words that bring the hell in the weeks to come that may get you carried away. You've heard me speak many times of the "Penis Principle." You're now old enough to know it simply means a man's intelligence is in direct opposition to his libido or sexual arousal. In other words, the harder your penis is, the lower your I.Q. will be. There is a right time and place for everything. Sex at your age and/or being unmarried is neither.

Scientists tell us other than the urge to eat, the urge to procreate is one of the strongest natural urges that exists.

Using this information to uncontrollably succumb to either urge leads to unnecessary health risks. Think for a moment how you would feel if your doctor, after giving you your annual physical, were to tell you, you have AIDS. Unfortunately, at least 5,000 people will have that conversation today. The number 5,000 is a lot of people. Would you want to be one of them? Of course not. But put yourself in the wrong situation and you'll make yourself a candidate. We've already discussed how you can't get that day, time, or moment back.

While we're discussing feelings, estimate your emotional stability immediately after receiving the news that little, "Bump and Grind," you and R. Kelly didn't see anything wrong with in Aquanetta's basement, has produced a 7lbs. 10 0z., baby boy. Are you ready? It doesn't matter. Girlfriend has had a baby and with a baby comes a mountain of responsibilities. Oh, you can duck them, claim the child isn't yours, or she should have "handled" it or taken the proper precautions, but the fact remains there's another person on this earth and you helped bring them here. How would you feel if your father disowned you? How would you like it if he ignored the fact you existed by never calling, never coming to see you, not taking care of your needs, not thinking you were worth the trouble to work overtime for? (For those whose fathers did this, do you really want to doom your children to the hurt you faced?)

Now is a good time to review what a man is. A man is a male that is honest, reliable as well as self-reliant, and he assumes responsibility not only for his own actions, but for the actions of those people or <u>things</u> he is responsible for. His children are never hungry or naked, for he will work to feed and clothe them. His children will never hunger for love or attention" for he will be there to provide them with both. His children will know foolishness when they see it, for he will provide them with an example of what intelligence is.

Fathers are important. Fathers provide examples for boys on how to act and models for girls on what to expect. If you are a father, it is your job to ensure your child is safe and warm. If you are a father, your duty is to respect and honor life and all those who bring it. If you are a man" your mission is to prepare your loved ones for a comfortable life when you are gone.

Fatherhood is not something you can or should run from. Should it happen and you're not prepared, stand up straight, hold your head up, realize you have some sacrifices to make, and then make yourself legitimately dependable. Even when it occurs under the best circumstances, the same rules apply.

Any fool can help make a baby, but it takes a man to help take care of one. Points to consider whether you are at home, Middle School, High School, College or out on your own. Creating life calls for maturity, foresight, and responsibility because fatherhood will place demands that will fall squarely on your shoulders.

We have enough thugs. Fatherhood should be the only type of 'hood you aspire to and for the reasons I've just explained only then when you are ready.

Love,Dad

GOD

Dear Son,

I realize many times you may have heard someone refer to **GOD** yet you may have never inquired about HIM. Indeed, the concept of a being that knows all and sees all and is always with us yet we can't see HIM, may be a little too much for any one to understand. The very fact it's hard to comprehend acknowledges there are things beyond our capacity to explain. Mankind is a curious animal that sometimes is so egotistical, he must be able to explain everything. Yet a simple question like which came first, the chicken or the egg, can throw him into a tailspin.

Don't get me wrong; there are many things that can and should be explained. We have brains and those brains brought forth science. To be afraid to question and do the research, to dare to move beyond one's own comfort zone, would leave us in caves and animal skins. I see no harm in advancing reverently.

But it is hard for man, in all his vanity, to accept the fact he is not the be-all and end-all. To accept the fact something greater than he exists and keeps things together, created whatever needed to be created without the benefit of his opinion, and manages to keep it running without his sage advice is a bit much for us and our smart little selves.

Once we learn to get over ourselves, then we can advance reverently. To advance reverently is to realize we can do all things through Christ who strengthens us. From inventing the air conditioner to space travel. From designing the Interstate Highway system to developing the cure for Polio, Diphtheria, Diabetes, Cancer, and AIDS. To advance reverently is to accept **GOD** put us here now to do whatever he needs us to do even if we don't understand why. To advance reverently is to understand **GOD** wants us to have the knowledge to be all we can be, along with acquiring the wisdom to thank HIM for it.

Is there a being that knows all? Well, I don't believe in coincidences, so something or someone had to plan for things to work out a certain way. Is there a being that sees all? I believe in order for HIM to be where you needed HIM in order for HIM to help you, HE would at the very least have to have an extensive network of eyes, wouldn't HE?

Yet, say the skeptics, we can't see him. We can't see the air either, but we breathe. Like the wind, we can't see HIM. But like the wind, we can see what HE has done, is doing, and will do. Just because you don't see something doesn't mean it isn't there.

Would we know **GOD** if we saw HIM? Probably not, and I believe HE would prefer it that way. Think about it. If you don't know who **GOD** is, but you know you could meet HIM any moment, you're almost forced to be civil to everyone, aren't you? In fact, in the bible there is a passage about being kind to strangers because they may be Angels in disguise. Once again we are being encouraged to be cordial. What is the harm in that?

Admittedly there are people that doubt the existence of **GOD** completely. If HE exists, why would he allow decent people to get into bad accidents, die from heart attacks and disease or just have a hard time when the lowdown folks do whatever they want? How is it the Pastor can say stand your feet and thank **GOD** for waking you up this morning but two minutes later when he tells the congregation Sister So and So died in her sleep and went home to be with the Lord, she's now in a better place?

It's as confusing to me as it is to you. I think it may be about being thankful with whatever you have, no matter what situation you are in. You know, doing the best you can with what you have.

Think about it for a moment and imagine the encouragement you may provide for that individual who was feeling sorry for himself until he saw you and what you had to go through. Suddenly it would dawn on him he has no excuses because things could be worse. Now before you start emceeing your own "Pity Party," you've got to realize there are folks out there who would love to be in your shoes. Speaking of shoes, whenever I used to sing a "woe is me" song, I remember your Grandmother telling me, "I once complained of having no shoes until I saw a man with no feet." Get it? Someone somewhere has it worse than you so take what you have that works and win with that.

You'll make mistakes but that's okay. Every brand new morning is **GOD'S** way of saying, "get up, go try it again, and do it right this time." Those times when you feel all alone are **GOD'S** way of saying, "It's time for us to talk," if you'll listen. Listen to the voice that is telling you to do something that will help someone other than yourself or your particular group. That's **GOD** talking to you. Listen to the voice that is saying to do something that is right, not because it's popular, but because it's the right thing to do. That's **GOD** talking to you. Listen to the voice that says no one is watching, but do the right thing anyway. The truth is, someone is always watching. The devil will flood you with opportunities to do the right thing, and **GOD** will make sure the right person sees what YOU chose to do. Then, you know what? You will have provided an example of what a good man is and your example will encourage another, who will encourage another, and so on and so on.

There are those that will ask, "how do we know **GOD** gives us anything or even exists for that matter? I feel **GOD'S** work whenever a golden Sunday afternoon in the summer or Saturday evening in the fall embraces me with a rush of energy and expectation. I hear **GOD'S** voice in the rush of the wind in winter or the hush of a breeze in spring. I witness **GOD'S** presence when sunlight beams through stained glass windows or moonlight makes an ocean, lake or river dance. I see **GOD** when I observe the cycle of a fall harvest that will give way to the cold winter only to have the rain from spring soften what winter made hard so we all can enjoy the summer. I see **GOD** when I look at you and realize you are me all over again, but a much newer, improved version. There are so many different beliefs on what **GOD** is, who **GOD** looks like, and who HE likes best. Looking at Christianity alone, the denominations or different groups are stifling. There are Lutherans, Presbyterians, Methodists, United Methodists, Calvinists, Episcopalians, Baptists, Free Will Baptists, Southern Baptists, Missionary Baptists, Pentecostals, Jehovah's Witnesses, African Methodist Episcopalians, African Methodist Episcopalian Zionists, Catholics, Irish Catholics, Roman Catholics and I know I'm leaving a whole lot of folks out.

They all seem to believe in **GOD** and **HIS SON, JESUS.** After that, everyone seems to go their own separate way. Some of them believe if you don't pray, sing, shout, kneel, speak in tongues, dress, or offer the same way they do, you're a candidate for the fires of Hell. Religion has been used to keep a people enslaved, lift up lowly spirits, bring down bank accounts, suppress civil uprisings, shame governments into doing the right thing and heal drug addicts. Like money or guns, to determine if it's bad or not depends on what you choose to use it for.

Members of the congregation, flock, or believers meet regularly in a Mosque, Temple, Church, Cathedral, or House to listen to their Rabbi, Imam, Leader, Pastor, Minister, Bishop, Overseer, Elder, Priest, Father, Brother, Sister or Holy Woman give his or her interpretation of what **GOD** would have you know this week.

It's interesting how you can go to the right neighborhood and see a church and a liquor store on every other corner. I've often wondered why, if they all believe in love and Christmas, don't they get together once a month, pool their resources and force banks, insurance and real estate companies to help them start businesses and build homes.

Isn't it amazing how the same people that bend over backwards trying to be nice and warm and fuzzy in the church are the same ones who will curse you out if you have them blocked in in the parking lot because they have to hurry up and get on with the rest of their day?

You know, I've always believed church on Sunday was nothing more than practice for the big game you play Monday through Saturday. In other words, jumping up and down and whooping and hollering or rocking back and forth or whispering amen in your most dignified voice is just a wasted effort if you are not showing that love, justice, patience, kindness, forgiveness, faith and stewardship Monday through Saturday. Small wonder the late Lenny Bruce said, "Everyday more and more people are straying from the church and going back to **GOD**."

You're old enough now to figure out everything that says its holy, isn't and the devil can quote scripture as well as any Pope. Like anything else life can show us, the real proof of one's substance lies in the acts he performs, his actions. Not in the lies he tells during a performance. Character is doing the right thing when no one is looking. Allow your spiritual leader to be someone with character, not someone who *is* a character.

Read and study your bible so you can learn more about and get to know **GOD** for yourself. Get to know HIM well enough to trust HIM. This means not having a problem saying grace (giving thanks for the food) in McDonald's or questioning what you don't understand. Be kind but don't be gullible. Be patient but don't be a doormat. Be forgiving while keeping in mind the guilty party might commit the same act again, and, if you must, forgive again, then put some distance between you two.

Look for the good in everything and the **GOD** will come out in you.

Remember those people that tell you about **GOD** are telling you what *they* see. They are not **GOD**. Too many confuse **GOD** with the person that's bringing the message from HIM. They think getting close to the messenger will get them closer to **GOD**. A Pastor's most important job is to bring the word from **GOD**. Give them all the respect they're due, but when is the last time you've seen a Temple erected to a mailman? They bring the message. They carry the mail. They're human and mess up like everyone else. Putting this as plainly as I can, don't worship them. Worship **GOD**.

Karl Marx once said, "Religion is the opiate of the masses." There will always be nay-sayers and non-believers. What is important is what you believe. Will a man's religious beliefs determine his values or do his values determine his religious beliefs? I'll leave that determination to you. I'll only ask you to respect the beliefs of others so long as those beliefs don't hurt any other living thing.

The more you study your chosen denomination, the more peace you should find when you reflect upon its meaning. If, through study, no peace arrives, perhaps you should study something else. This is another one of those areas I must stress you do for you. In other words, don't just go along with the crowd. Everyone is to develop their own personal relationship with their GOD. It's okay to pray *for* someone, but they should also know how to pray for themselves.

Question. Seek. Search.

A prayer has been called many things. From talking to GOD to making requests, every prayer can be composed of one of the following, but the complete prayer should contain all of the following- *Praise*- though nothing more than saluting your GOD as your Creator and benefit maker with a joyful shout or a reverent nod, seems difficult for some to offer; *Thanksgiving*- remembering to include a thank you for the little things we tend to overlook but would be lost without like sight, the ability to walk, hearing and our good common sense; *Intercession*- seeking aid or requesting something for someone else; *Asking*- when making a request its helpful to remember a "no" or "not yet" from GOD is always in our best interest and finally; *Forgiveness*- all have sinned, not just y'all, therefore try to keep in mind all (including and especially you), not just y'all, need to be forgiven.

Can you afford to be judged with the same measuring stick you use to judge others? The work we send out today will return ten times to either bless or blaspheme us or our descendants, tomorrow. Always be kinder, more gracious, and classier than anyone expects you to be.

Love, Dad

Comforting Ill Loved Ones

Dear Son,

At one time or another in your life you may be called upon to help an injured or ill friend or relative recuperate. Everyone imagines they'll do the "right" thing at the right time or they'll be "there" for whoever needs them because that's "just the thing to do." But what does it really mean to take care of someone who is in pain and incapable of doing the things they ordinarily would do for themselves? We'd all like to believe it's in our nature to be supportive, but I've found those words are easier said than done.

I have had the good fortune to be around more than a few people who were quite happy in their independence. They could come and go as they pleased until something, an accident or disease knocked them totally off their feet. They're usually angry because they have to depend on someone else for assistance. Sometimes, they take out their anger on the very people trying to assist them. I would be angry too because I felt they shouldn't be ill and I couldn't do a damned thing about it.. That's at least two people angry over circumstances they cannot immediately control. Both sides want the injured party back the way they were.

The key, in this case, is to focus on what "is" and not what "was." Prayerfully, the injured or ill person will convalesce (or heal) to the point they come back with their independence intact. The question is, on the way back to that, what can I do to make them comfortable in the mean time? Walking around angry and sucking my teeth every time they asked me to do something didn't help and only made them feel worse for asking in the first place. It made me feel worse for getting an attitude when what I should have been giving was assistance. Words like patience, smile, help and effort come to mind when I think of how to comfort someone I care about who is in pain. Say these words to yourself before you see the ill person, not after.

It took me awhile, but I finally figured out sometimes all you can offer is a hand to hold, a shoulder for support or a genuine encouraging word with your time. You'll notice I said, "with your time." Sitting in a sick person's room constantly glancing at your watch as if you had to spend an exact amount of time in order for your visit to be legitimate, only irritates you both. Be there because you want to be there and let your actions; not your words, show that. Don't count the minutes, make the minutes count. Don't ask how they feel because frankly, if they felt alright they wouldn't be where they are in the first place. Try to be the best part of their day.

Some people try your patience when they're ill. Do what you can to be supportive, make sure they have what you can afford to give them when you leave, and then come back to assure them we're going through this together. Ask them what they would like. Ask them what they would like to do. You may have to read to them, lotion their feet or cut their meat. Someone once did this for you and when they did it, it was considered a labor of love. Think of this as your opportunity to return the favor.

Love, Dad

Death

Dear Son,

Everything that is alive either grows or it dies. There are no exceptions. I once asked your Grandmother what death was. She said it just means a person's spirit leaves this world and goes to either Heaven or Hell. Of course I asked what a spirit was. She said it was what made you what you were. Your spirit fills your body like water fills a glass. Once the water is poured from this particular container, the glass becomes useless.

How you live determines whether or not you go to Heaven or Hell. The dictionary calls death the end of life; the total and permanent cessation of all the vital functions of an animal or plant. The last time was your last chance. That goodbye we played with was for real.

Baptists say when someone you love dies, if they have asked the Lord Jesus to be their personal Savior, you will see them again in Heaven if you have done the same. That may be true, but there is nothing like the sense of utter despair you feel when you realize you won't see that person again alive in this life. I guess that's part of the reason I wrote this book for you. I knew if I never saw you again, there was still so much we had to talk about and it just wouldn't be fair to leave you hanging with no one to answer your questions. As it has been laid upon my heart to make sure you don't feel left out or apart from the other guys whose fathers were with them all the time, we can share these letters that were written specifically for you. I'm proud you're taking the time to read this and I'm proud of you. You are my responsibility. I am responsible for you and to you.

You have no idea how much it pleases me that you are reading this letter. It means you have me whenever you need me. You know, it's amazing how much we take for granted in our lives. Because we've known them for as long as we can remember, we expect friends and family to be there forever. We may even try to imagine what life would be like if they were gone. No matter how much you imagine, it's always ten times worse when it's real. When his mother died, Pastor Weathers asked me if you ever get over your mother dying. I told him no, you just learn to live with it.

How would you treat a dear friend or relative if you knew next week you would be attending their funeral? Differently, huh? My guess is we would all be a lot more considerate, the hugs would last longer, the smiles would be genuine, the nuisances would be nullified, and our talks and time would contain a lot more substance.

Now how do you know that dear friend or relative won't be gone next week? The fact is, you don't. Before my father died from injuries sustained in a car accident, he left the house saying, "see ya later sport." It was a regular day with nothing out of the ordinary. I never saw him alive again.

My mother had breast cancer that caused her health to slowly deteriorate. Here was the only woman who could beat me running, the woman that taught me how to read and act, the woman who made sure I never had a bad Christmas or birthday, too weak to breathe.

I suppose what I'm saying is, I've seen death come both ways fast and slow and neither is better when it's someone that you love. When they died, I felt like the world should stop turning, but it didn't. As much as we don't want it to, life goes on. The world will keep turning. That doesn't mean we shouldn't grieve. We should. We must. When someone tells you they're sorry about your loss, just say thank you and go on from there. While you may occasionally reminisce, you cannot spend the rest of your life looking back. What I'm saying is, be wise enough to appreciate the things you can do and the people you have in your life now while you can. Make every day count and every relationship special. Take no one for granted because you'll only be granted a short period of time. Always do the best you can with what you have and if you must be known for something, let it be that you stood for the right things.

I believe we should treat everyone like we would want to be treated, do what we say we're going to do and remember we can't always determine where we came from, but we can always decide where we're going. If you can get excited about where you are right now and fill each moment with meaning, you'll never be bored.

Realize you had help every step of the way to a triumph and the times when it seems you're most alone are times GOD wants you all to HIMSELF to talk to. A loss isn't really a loss if you've learned something from it. After every adventure and especially after every failure, ask yourself, "What have we learned from this experience?" If we've learned something, anything, the event was not a waste.

Live and love as though you were going to die tomorrow, but learn and reach as though you were going to live forever. Need further instructions? Check "Dad's Rules of Engagement."

It is said we are born to die. Well, I've just explained to you the best way to die, by living your way out. If you can do this, when it's time to die, you'll be willing to go on to the next phase, whatever it is, knowing this life was time, well spent. Why? Because in doing all these things you can't help but leave the place a little better than the way you found it. Then, its on to the next phase.

What is the next phase? I cling to the belief it's Heaven. To me, Heaven is a place you go to in the blink of an eye, the taking of a breath. You go there so fast there's no time to look back. Heaven is where all your questions are answered and pancakes and barbecue sandwiches are served 24 hours a day.

It is further than far yet closer than right here. It is a place you're allowed to witness the highlights and lowlights of your life and those times you thought nobody saw. While you watch, you're constantly being reminded you had a choice. Whether or not you sought forgiveness for your actions determines whether or not you get to stay.

You get to go to a warehouse filled with your heart's desires that somehow, you never got. It is then you're told these are the things that were set aside for you and you alone that you would have gotten, if only you had had a little more faith in GOD.

I will tell you as I have told others. You will make mistakes. Learn from them. When life knocks you down, pick yourself up, dust yourself off and go try to do the right thing again and again and again. Remember, you are the star of your life's story and the film is running. If you allow your GOD to be the director, it will be an award winning production.

When you hear of my passing, know these things; I tried my best to make sure you knew you were so special you couldn't be left out, forgotten or left behind and I leave you this book as your constant reference. I want you to go on and live your dreams. I'll be spending half of my time watching GOD unfold the mysteries of the universe and the other half reuniting with my parents and meeting those ancestors I had only heard about (you know, the ones on the family reunion tee shirt), I care about you and lastly, I love you too much to just sit back and let you be sorry.

I'll be awaiting the day you join us with your news of the great things you have done.

Love, Dad

Your Own Pursuit of Excellence

Dear Sons,

There will come a time when you will find you have amassed enough knowledge through your life's experiences to establish your own set of principles. This will be the defining moment you make known to the world what you will and will not stand for; what is negotiable and what is not, what is unacceptable and what is up for debate.

This will be the set of rules you have chosen to live by. Allow me to caution you to make them as realistic as possible; for if you should ever choose to retreat from them, you will find it progressively easier to question things you said you believe in. Once this occurs, your self-confidence will erode and your enemies will leap at the opportunity to expose your reversal of will to any that might listen.

Here are my principles, mind you, I said mine, so that you may have an example both of what principles are and how what they are, provide a better explanation of why we are the way we are. Speak up for those who are either afraid to or can't. Treat people like you would want to be treated. Give audience to responsible views that differ from yours. Love like it's your last time. Learn like you'll live forever. Live with as few regrets as possible. Remember where you come from. Say what you mean and mean what you say. Don't get in it if you're not trying to win it. Think higher.

Accurately survey the room, audience, class, group, crowd, or terrain, then encourage, debate, admonish, rebuke, observe, pray, sing, whisper, inquire, lead, follow, or shut up. Make the words you are about to speak pass through at least two of the three gates; Are the words true? Are the words kind? Are the words necessary?

Always be that tough act to follow. That means leave before someone has to tell you to go and when they see you returning, the good people should smile. Never announce your plans to everyone. Some folks may not have your best interests at heart. Know that your GOD loves you so much he had a guy you may never meet sit down and write a book just for you so you couldn't be left out.

Always remember the Devil is a liar that knows exactly what you like. Deals with him or his representatives will take you further than you wish to go, detain you longer than you wish to stay, and cost you more than you wanted to pay. In other words, get in bed with the Devil, and you're going to get screwed. The ends do not justify the means. That simply means if you cannot get what you want without breaking the law or needlessly hurting someone, you really don't need it.

If you always do what you've always done, you always get what you've always got. That's almost fine if you always win. I say almost because if you always win, perhaps the victories are coming too easily and easy victories are never cherished. Easy victories make us think we're better than we really are. Easy victories set us up for hard losses. If you always win, perhaps the level of competition isn't what it should be. Challenge yourself to improve. Read and finish a book a month. Learn different foreign languages. Devote your personal time to a charity. We've already covered when you should fight. Help someone who is struggling to do the right thing. With every worthwhile endeavor, there is struggle. Nothing of value is ever gained without it. It reveals a person's true character, it forms unbreakable bonds, and give one a greater sense of respect for the accomplishments of others. It is that prize you win when you've waged war with everything you have within you; your wits, your strength, your intelligence, and your faith, that has exhausted all you are and taught you just what you are, that you will prize above all else. Why? Because you had to work for it! You must set a standard for yourself and never go below it. If you do, you will find it progressively easier to take the low road and just get by and when it comes to working for something you really care about you'll find yourself out of condition for the battle. We are warriors, you and I, but in our fight to make the world a better place for all let's not forget to have fun. It can be done, you know. I wrote a poem about it. Like to hear it? Here it go

-One Glorious Season In The Sun They Sought
To Take Wings Of Victorious Flight
So They Girded Their Loins And Steadied Their
*   Nerves*
And Focused On The Challenge In Sight
With Passion, Sweat, And Unwavering Calm
They Vanquished Each Quite Startled Foe
Who Cursed And Cried And Pitied Themselves
And The Triumph That They Would Not Know
Who Dares Approach Victory So Loudly
With A Roar, A Swagger, And A Wink?
Said We, 'Tis Us And We've Something To Prove
And That's We're A Lot Better Than You Think!
And When We Left With The Trinket That Read
*   "Champion"*
With A Wink That Revealed This Was Fun
We Turned To Thank The Almighty
For One Glorious Season In The Sun....

Excellence is something that must be pursued. Although it's rarely ever captured or held for long, we often find our efforts to attain it and the journey toward it, have made us and those in our company, better persons.

Deepest Love and Admiration,
The guy who wouldn't leave anyone behind

.

Dad's Rules of Engagement

Engagement (en gaj` ment), n. 1. The act of engaging.

7. An encounter, conflict, or battle.

1. Talk with GOD regularly.

2. Never waste time.

3. Remember, with the proper preparation or carelessness, anything can be taken.

4. Choose your battles carefully. Don't fight about everything.

5. When you do choose to speak, make the words worth hearing.

6. Envision life as a suspect, it will keep you from becoming a victim.

7. Occupy your brain with turning the impossible into reality.

8. Think with your mouth closed.

9. Consider the messenger and the message.

10. Always be kinder, more gracious, and classier than anyone expects you to be.

11. Set goals, timetables, and deadlines.

12. A smile offers encouragement and lowers the defenses.

13. Speak the truth but do not expect it in return.

14. Know enough to say you don't know enough.

15. Force is never used unless it is overwhelming and has clear, achievable goals.

16. Do not cheat or steal.

17. Make informed decisions.

18. Listen to your Guardian Angel.

19. Always be a tough act to follow.

20. Always consider the cost of the victory.

21. Prepare your loved ones for your eventual departure.

22. Remember, if you don't make plans for yourself, someone will make plans for you.

23. Never lean on any person or thing you are not familiar with.

24. Observe strange acting people, animals and things from a safe distance.

25. Discipline yourself and no one else will ever have to.

Our Side-Words on the Subjects from the Subjects

The Importance of Role Models
By Trevor Germany

Being Spiritual
By Sean Fendall, Jr.

Becoming the Next Generation of Leaders
By Carrington Wells

A Newlywed and a Husband
By Carlton Fludd

A Son on the Importance of Fatherhood
By Maurice A. Banks IV

The Importance of Role Models

At some point in our lives there was someone we idolized. Someone we wanted to be just like. Some people find their role models at a very young age. We even recognize them as we get older. Sometimes, we don't even know who our role model may be. Subconsciously, we mimic the actions, faces, moods, and behaviors of these people. All this is done without guidelines or rules to help to discover your role model. So how is it we decide? Truth be told, there are no rules, nor an unwritten book that says someone may or may not be your role model. In fact you have complete control over who you decide to be your driving force, your inspiration, motivation, your ROLE MODEL. Everyone has their own reason or story behind their choice. I am an 18-year-old male in my first year of college and it couldn't be anymore obvious to me who my role model is. For starters she is a Woman. A strong black woman, that is. This lady has been through so much and yet she still finds ways to make ends meet. My MOM has been there for me since I can remember. We don't always see eye to eye but she's always there. My mom had me when she was 16 years old. Yes, she was still in high school, eleventh grade to be exact. She still managed to graduate on time. My mom was raised by a single mother.

She is and always has been a single parent. I'm the oldest of three. I have two younger sisters.

My family is very active. Both my younger sisters are involved in extra curricular activities. The younger of my two sisters, runs track, and is a cheerleader. The oldest one also runs and dances. They both maintain excellent grades. So I ask myself, "Why does everything seem so normal?" Homes that some people call "broken" don't always follow a script or justify the statistics. I guess when you have such a force driving your home from the inside the idea of becoming a successful family is only an unexpected surprise to outsiders.

I have a woman for a role model. I always figured your role model was supposed to be your favorite sports figure. As a male, you would expect a Super hero, even an older sibling of some sort, not a lady. Well once again I'm not following the statistics. My mom is my role model.

A role model is supposed to be someone you look up to. Someone you admire, a person you respect heavily because they have done something to earn this level of respect you have for them. My mother is phenomenal. She does for my sisters and I when all odds are against her. She has constantly instilled great morals and values in my life. She is a constant driving force in the decisions I make daily. Above all else, she takes care of herself. She practices what she preaches. She is a person that leads by example. She is a mother, friend, and mentor all in one.

Don't be just like your role model.... Be better. That's what I was told. In some ways it makes sense. For someone to be your role model, they obviously must have done something right in your eyes. So why not be even better than them? Push your self to achieve what they haven't.

In conclusion, I'm just saying find someone whose good examples work for you. There's no book on choosing a role model. Anyone can be one, but know that they're special. Once that special person is found, everything they do is viewed as heroic. They're loved. They have showed you what you believe is the right way.

Making them your role model is your way of promising them that you'll be just as good as they are or better. You're promising them that you'll fight just as hard they did, then achieve more. That is the promise I'm making to my mother.

Trevor Germany is a high school graduate and a freshman in college.

BEING SPIRITUAL

I believe that spirituality is one of the key points in a young man's life. These present times, with their various distractions and temptations, make it hard for young men in the world today. That is why I am so thankful for the relationship I have with my Lord and Savior Jesus the Christ. It is much easier to deal with the mess in the world when you have spiritual support. Some of my peers think that they have no purpose in life. Then there are those young men who have a spiritual relationship with their God to the point theirs is a purpose driven life. That is why it is so important that when you find your purpose in life and you move into the calling that God has on your life, you use your gift for God's glory and not for selfish praise. Make sure that the calling (your purpose) is really what God has called you to do and not what you want to be called to do. One thing you should never do is try to base your spiritual relationship with God on what you see in the church because the church has some of the fakest people you will ever see in your life. One of my major problems with people in the church is some of them are always doing things for show and to be seen, not to glorify God. That is why the church is a mess now because everybody wants to do every thing except what God has called them to do. Some people in the church want to be over ministries trying to do everybody else's job and nobody is staying in their own lane. That is where all of the mess starts. That is why it is very important to stay prayed up about everything you do in spiritual relationship; Lord should I do this; Lord should I do that, because so many people lose focus. It seems to me when you have a spiritual relationship with God at a young age it will make you a better man. I say that because when you get older and you start dealing with the things that life throws at you, you will not try to handle things on your own. You will give it to God. At a young age some young men around me think that since they don't have any money they have to go out here and sell drugs. I say if you have a relationship with God you will see and be surprised how God will provide.

A key factor in a young man's life is who he has as a role model. I say this because there are a lot of young men whose fathers aren't there or don't they have males in their lives to look up to. That has a huge affect on the way they will turn out. When you choose a role model, make sure that you choose them for the positive things they do in life and not for the negative things. For example, if you choose your role model because they sell drugs and make a lot of money off of it, then you have your mind set that when you get older you want to do the same, but if you choose as your role model someone that has all of the fine things in life because they worked hard for them, when you get old, you will work for the things you want in life.

The role models in my life would have to be my father, Shawn Fendall Sr., Demitri Kornegay, William Posey Jr., Lorenzo Evans III., and Dobie Godbee. These men are my role models because they are men of God, they are hard, dedicated workers and most of them have families they provide for.

Providing for your family is a major characteristic for my role model because one day I want to have a family of my own and it is not always easy providing for your family, but my role models with families to provide for do a good job at it.

Shawn Fendall, Jr. is a sophomore at Douglass Senior High in Upper Marlboro, Maryland.

Becoming The Next Generation of Leaders

I am a young African American male who watches television, reads the news and surfs the net to get a better understanding of what's going on in the mainstream. By doing so, I'm always updated on what has occurred in the so called "real world". While being inundated with this abundance of information I have been able to determine for myself what a true leader is, what their characteristics are, and the qualities they should display. People may never agree whether a great leader is born or if a leader is made. As a young a black male, I definitely understand what is wrong with leaders today. My answer is nothing is wrong with leaders today, they're doing just fine, it is the youth whom don't listen to all of the great information that is being given. It seems as though the youth of today don't want to listen to the elders and leaders who know what they're talking about because of experience and research. No, today's youth want to experience life first hand and learn from their own mistakes. This way learning is sometimes fatal or at least life changing because of some drastically learned lessons. When it comes to me looking up to a leader, lots of things come to mind before I consider opinions and decide to follow them. First of all, I have to know if this particular leader can impact my life in a positive way. Then soon after that make sure he/she has leadership qualities they have developed through a never ending process of self-study, training, and outright experience. When someone decides if you're a good leader, they first observe you to see who you are and what you bring to the table. No matter where a leader lives or where they're from, they should always have good communication skills, the ability to work under pressure and possess the ability to effectively interact with a variety of different cultures and ethnic groups. A great leader allows people that they lead to have their own opinions and hears them out, he/she does not intentionally seek the lime light, won't let me give up, works as hard or harder than anyone else and corrects my performance in private.

The friends that I hang out with want the same things out of a leader as I do. Usually people who share the same interests or the same political views stick together and are close. My peers think that a leader should be all they can be and understand that they are responsible for whom ever they lead, which is very, very important.

While participating in a program called, Men Under Construction at my mother's church, I acquired a great deal of knowledge I didn't believe at the time was mandatory for me to know. As life progresses, I now know different. There were topics that piqued my interest so much that I had to ask those extra questions after things were said and done and class was over. Being a graduate of the program, I can gladly say that my oral communication has improved greatly since I first started, and I'm now able to step out, speak up and be a leader when ever it's necessary. I suppose a lot of males my age are frustrated because it's difficult to make our feelings known. I can and I'm considered a leader. All of this is possible because of the program and the program only. Every church ought to have a program like this.

Mainly because of all the positive male role models that have inspired me so much, I'm a leader. Want more leaders? Talk *to* us and not so much *about* us and we'll learn to listen, we'll learn to appropriately respond and there won't be the problems that are prominent in youth in today's society.

Carrington Wells is a senior at McKinlev Tech High in Washington, D.C.

A Newlywed and A Husband

I was married to my soul mate on June 11th 2005. I never at any time was nervous, scared or indecisive about being married, much less being married to her, because I knew she was the one for me. For me I would have been afraid of being married to someone that got on my nerves or that I could not stand. See, for me, I have always wanted to be married; ever since I graduated high school. For a lot of people this would hard to believe, but that is a true testament of being a product of your environment. Before my father's untimely death, my parents were married for 47 years. I always saw how my father related to my mother. He treated her with the utmost love and respect and he never raised his voice to her. He always put her first and would do just about anything to make her happy. He was a great husband and family man. He would go without to make sure his family was taken care of. As I was coming up as a young man, I would see my father do some of the grocery shopping and he would prepare all of the meals including Thanksgiving and Christmas. At one time, he had his own demolition company and I would hear him rustling through the house at 5:00 a.m. to prepare for another days work and on some weekends I would have to go to work with him, much to my dismay. When I graduated high school, I wanted to start working and get married, just like my father did, but as far as the getting married part, I was not as fortunate as my father. I dated quite a few women with little or no luck. As I matured, I realized that what I wanted when I was eighteen, wasn't what I wanted when I was twenty-eight. For example, when I was eighteen I wanted a *girl* that had a great big chest, big behind and a big smile. As I matured and went through a whole bunch of experiences, I realized that I needed a **woman** with some damn common sense! First I started making improvements on myself and I had to look no further than the **man** who raised me. Because my father was a shining example of what a man is to be, I felt the need to take a few pages from his book.

Because I had seen my father wake up early in the morning and prepare for work, it gave me the impression that that was what a man was supposed to do and how he should look after his household. I realized also, that he made me go to work with him so I could know how to get up a go to a job in the morning. He was preparing me for everyday life. I would see my father put love into all meals that he prepared, so that let me know that as a man, I can do the grocery shopping and prepare the meals to make sure my family is fed; dispelling the myth that women do all of the cooking. My father showed me how to fish and how to plant and grow a garden. So if nothing else, my family will have tomatoes, greens, squash, string beans and fish for dinner. In other words, my father taught me that a man provides for his family and can be self reliant if necessary. Because I was the last child, I never saw exactly how he raised my older brothers, but upon looking now, I see how he raised two powerful men to be prepare and that can be productive in today's society. I wouldn't dare taint that legacy by not stepping up to be the man that my father quietly taught us to become. I saw the love that he intentionally, unconditionally and deliberately gave to a wonderful woman in my mother, three upstanding men in me and my two brothers, two beautiful daughter-in-laws, three precious granddaughters and two handsome grandsons. I now have the ultimate template to become a better man, a better husband, son, uncle and when my wife and I start our family, a better father. The bar is raised extremely high, but now I am better prepared to jump over it.

In my wife I found an absolute treasure and gift. She is a testament that with prayer, patience and acceptance of my role as a man and what a man should be, I can accomplish and be a man for the ages. She is my cheerleader and my biggest hero! She is my heartbeat and the air I breathe. She is my biggest fan and she is on my court, dishing me the rock or giving the alley while I've got the oop! She deserves all of the love that I can give her and with the training and teachings that my father instilled in me, I feel confident that I can be the husband that she deserves.

Carlton Fludd is a native Washingtonian and a newlywed.

A Son On the Importance of Fatherhood

As an oldest son it is hard to miss how important a father is to a family and to a child. What I've learned about being a father is that he has to be able to take on several roles to raise his children. In my life my father has been my coach, my doctor, tutor, my mentor, my role model, my pastor, my accountant and my Dad. Along with taking on these roles a father has to be able to create an environment that gives his child potential to be safe and to grow as a person. I also learned that it is a father's obligation to give to his children the tools to one day survive on their own and become a Dad themselves.

As a child I was taught the basics to not only survive in life, but to survive in his house. As a boy in my house the rules were made very clear of what was expected and what was not accepted. I've learned that being clear and upfront is a vital ingredient in raising a child and being a good father. In my house, we are taught to respect our elders, protect our mother, and defend our family. Simply put, these rules kept me in a house and out of trouble. As a boy there was a low tolerance for deviation from these rules. My father has been an essential guide and aide to help me become who I am. He has always shown me the right direction to be successful at whatever it was I was doing. My father has done all he could to make sure that whatever it was that I wanted to do I could be as good as I could doing it. He has spent countless hours coaching me in football, basketball, and baseball. As well as spending numerous dollars sending me to camps, and clinics to help me get better. As I child he paid for me to learn the piano and would never let me quit because he saw that there was potential for me to good piano player. This is how my father is with every part of my life. He is always right behind me pushing me to be as good as possible.

My father has also created a community around me to help shape who I am. He made sure that I was surrounded by people, especially men, who believed in God and could provide counsel and support for me throughout my life. I have several uncles who have all made sure they had a hand in coaching and counseling me. I have had strong influential men around me all my life because of my father. He created a positive environment that kept me in the right direction.

There has always been one uncle that has shown me how to be a leader for most of my life. Since a young age my uncle has always believed that I was a special person and has always given advice and congratulations through out each stage of my life. He has also been there to push me and let me know that if I could envision myself doing it, then it was possible.

Another way my father has created an environment is through my faith in God. In his house we are not forced, but we are raised in the church allowing us to find God for ourselves. This is one of the most helpful tools my father has ever given me. I say this because there comes a time when you can't do things on your own and you don't know how you'll make it and there is no one there to help you. This is when my faith in God allows me to find a way. When "my" father is not around, "Our" father is. Because my father can not be there with me at all times helping me every step of the way, he knows that I am protected and in the right hands at all times.

To me, my father has been my key to success. He has always let me know that as long as I was being positive and productive he would be there to support me in anyway he could. My father and the community of fathers he created for me have set great examples on how to be a father. They have all shown me how a father affects lives through his children when they try to raise them as best they can because they take just as much pride in our success as we do.

Maurice A. Banks IV is a graduate of Georgetown University.

Printed in the United States
83076LV00003B/199-1500/A

9 781602 666115